HURRICANE

Storm Side Patriots
One Voice, One Nation, One God

FACTOR

MICA MOSBACHER

Publisher:
Elite Online Publishing
63 East 11400 South #230
Sandy, UT 84070
www.EliteOnlinePublishing.com

Printed in the United States of America

ISBN-13: 978-1-5136-2637-6

This book is dedicated to my late husband Bob, and to my amazing son Cameron Duncan, and to my precious grandchildren Donnie and Harris. It is also written for the glory of God.

'I can do all things through Him Who Strengthens Me."
-Philippians 4:13

Contents

PROLOGUE

How big is your storm? I grew up hearing countless sermons about overcoming the storms of life. The Bible includes recurring themes of adversity, trials, suffering and waiting on God's abundant blessings. The book of Mark cites the story of Jesus and His disciples who encounter a terrible squall while on a boat in the Sea of Galilee. The fishermen onboard were afraid but Jesus reassured them and God guided them to a safe shore. Jesus had asked the men 'where was your faith 2; and, calmed the seas."

When riding out adversity or a storm in life, sometimes our only refuge is faith in God Almighty. One of my favorite quotes is by Andre Gide: "You can never cross the ocean until you have the courage to lose sight of the shore." Fear and faith go hand in hand and our best navigation tools are turning to scripture and prayer during times of ultimate testing. It's when we are broken that God lets the light in.

The "storms of life" took on a whole new meaning in 2017 when a trio of three catastrophic storms - Harvey, Irma and Maria - pushed everyone in theirs paths to the ultimate limit. It tested the faith of believers, regardless of religious affiliation and took no prisoners.

For the estimated 13 million Texans adversely impacted by Harvey's powerful punch, it seemed like an eternity before God calmed the storm. Harvey forced dire 11th hour heroic rescues from homes, vehicles and businesses. There were frantic evacuations. Many turned their back on their homes and fled with the mere clothing on their backs. For a long while, it surely seemed like the mighty wind and water were triumphing over God's omnipotent power.

The cry by Captain Smith on the Titanic was alleged to be "Every man for himself - Abandon ship." While thousands of Texans abandoned their homes, no one abandoned them. Hurricane Harvey like an attention-seeking narcissist, certainly garnered national attention. As a result, people opened their hearts and their wallets, and assistance and resources poured into Texas and Louisiana.

There were hundreds of amazing acts of courage and compassion present both during and after the storm. Acts of kindness and unselfishness were on display everywhere. First responders put others first. They were the unsung heroes. Media story after media story highlighted the selfless acts of U.S. Coast Guard members and others. President Donald Trump praised the U.S. Coast Guard, the National Guard, the U.S. Army Corps of Engineers, fire and police departments, medical teams and linemen.

In the wake of the storm, armies of volunteers from legions of non-profits descended into the Gulf Coast Region like ants at a picnic. The Salvation Army and the American Red Cross swung into action. During Harvey alone, the Red Cross provided 4.5 million meals and 435,000 shelter stays along with their partners.

Men, women and children were battle-tested to the limit. Many relied on their faith to see them through an anguishing time. Harvey and its destruction did not break their spirits. The storm brought out the best in people. On proud display was America's core values and principles. Decency, courage, humor, compassion, selflessness and cooperation were evident on the war weary faces. The collective cooperation among perfect strangers of all origins and walks of life is the **Hurricane Factor**. Just showing up is the **H Factor**. At the end of the day it is about the greater good and extending a loving helping hand.

And, just when the collective Federal agencies and response teams were at their breaking point, along came Irma. An epic storm, it pounded Florida and the Keys took a direct hit. Once again, an exhausted overextended brigade of first responders answered the call of duty. Linemen and the Army Corps of Engineers were in overdrive.

While some areas were spared, other parts of the city resembled river reservoirs. Irma's prima donna tirades were wild and untamed.

Finally the sun came out, and it looked like the coast was clear. States were trying to find a way to bounce back. Texas Strong and Florida Strong were like battle cries. Spirits were sagging but resiliency and optimism was triumphing. All seemed brighter, and the long road to recovery had begun. And then, Maria reared its ugly head. There is an old wive's tale that warns bad things come in threes. And so it was.

Some might have wondered where was God? However, all one had to do was witness one or two examples of incredible kindness to realize that God was everywhere. I volunteered with the American Red Cross at the George R. Brown Convention Center and was touched by the concern of its army of volunteers. I helped serve food and was inspired to see the touching expressions of grateful hearts. Optimism was everywhere.

Soon, the hurricane season passed, and there was a national collective sigh of relief. Yet, God tested us again because the unthinkable happened. On October 1, 2017, a deranged gunman opened fire on innocent celebratory concert goers on the Las Vegas strip in Nevada. The carnage included 58 people dead - many young victims with their whole lives ahead of them. Promises, futures wiped out in minutes.

Loved ones were left reeling. The survivors, including 851 injured, would find their lives altered forever. This storm of life shattered the sense of safety and wellbeing at open air concerts. Yet once again, there were countless acts of courage among the first responders and attendees.

And then on November 5th, there was another shooting. This time, it was a mass shooting at the First Baptist Church in Sutherland Springs, Texas. The mentally-ill gunman killed 26 innocent people and injured 20 more. Many were children.

My close friend, former judge and DC area lawyer, Travis Lucas, introduced me by phone to one of the pastors whose church had been a staging scene. Pastor Paul is the minister at River Oaks Baptist church. A former police officer and missionary, he is a powerful voice of God. I went to meet him in Sutherland Springs, and he shared with me the powerful sermon he had preached on the Sunday following the shootings.

His community was grieving, and he sought to explain the unexplainable. God's ultimate, eternal triumph over evil was the only explanation. A leap of faith is required to cope and a belief in the hereafter. I felt that Pastor Paul's sermon would be appropriate for this book as it provides a blueprint for navigating the inexplicable suffering that follows acts of nature or despicable acts of mentally ill human beings that we have no control over.

When I conceived the idea for this book, I asked a friend of mine, former USAF Captain, meteorologist and former FBI Special Agent Mike Sharkey, to give me a "back of the napkin" explanation of the science behind the formation of hurricanes. He walked me through cyclones, wind currents, and counter clockwise and clockwise wind speeds. His explanation was technical and clinical. It was hard to describe a storm's impact on human lives.

Hearing firsthand from survivors and hurricane veterans who shared their often heartbreaking stories in their own words was compelling and personal. It was tough to pick and choose which raw stories to highlight. There were so many. It was overwhelming to comb through FaceBook and media stories to choose those to include.

I have in-laws and relatives who are police officers and firefighters. Some are the most dedicated I know, including former NYPD detectives Jaime Gonsales and Keith Schiller. Having served in an exemplary role at the Trump White House, Keith is in a class by himself. It is my honor to know such fine people. I focused on several first responders and officers in the book. Their big hearts touched me to the core. I count, as friends, several active and retired FBI agents, and first responders who are some of the most dedicated men and women I know.

Friends Mike Campi (retired FBI supervisor) and his wife Nancy helped out a young firefighters family after his home was impacted by Hurricane Sandy. His daughter Kaitlyn learned of the family who were affected in New Jersey. They were in a tough situation. The Campi family unofficially adopted them. They gave them money and supplies, and Nancy even made curtains. This is the "softer" side of the law enforcement that is a best kept secret.

I am therefore sharing an inspiring collection of voices in the storms. Each individual story includes an element of faith and resilience. The stories of strangers helping strangers also echoed and amplified The **Hurricane Factor.** Help was unconditional. No one asked a neighbor or stranger what church or synagogue he attended or what was his ethnic origin or political party. Helping hands did not hesitate to reach out.

It became apparent to me that Republicans helped Democrats during the many crises illustrated in this book. My concern is that we are tearing apart the very soul and the fabric of this nation with divisions. There is deep distrust and intolerance in opposite camps. It no longer seems that the public can engage in any civil dialogue. If a person is a dissenting voice, he becomes the enemy.

As this book was going to press, Senator John McCain died on August 25th, a few days before his 82nd birthday. He was a war hero, maverick and a man of deep personal convictions. He voted his principals and managed to reach across the aisle and win friends despite differences on policy. He was a hurricane force in the Senate.

My husband and I were deeply involved in his run for the presidency in 2008. Presidents Bush and Obama had heartfelt eulogies at his funeral services. He reached across the aisle and strived to do the right thing. Whether One agreed with him or not, his life story is inspirational and of service to mankind. His patriotism and belief that "more unites us than divides us" Is an exemplary example of the **H Factor.**

President Trump, per Senator Cruz, " threw a hand grenade into the Washington establishment." He harnessed hurricane force winds of change in the U.S. He tapped into the inferno of anger in this country and the deep distrust of the swamp in Washington, DC.

These men are the great disrupters of our century. It's human nature to be resistant to change and there are many who obstruct and resist. The prevailing winds in our country of hatred have been unleashed. The spirit of doing the right thing is being crushed. We are at the end of the day, all storm side patriots who are trying to feed our families and live our lives. We all want the same things. " Life, liberty and the pursuit of happiness.

When I get off a tv news channel, I am appalled by the vile personal attacks and insults I often receive via twitter. It's laughable at times but also deeply disturbing. Is this who we are becoming as a society? Also deeply disturbing is the needless identity politics and a certain fueling by some MSM outlets regarding racism.

I spent some of my childhood in Memphis, Tennessee. I had the distinct privilege of hearing Martin Luther King. I still quote his words on the air. "Hate begets hate - violence begets violence - toughness begets a greater toughness. We must meet the forces of hate with the power of love."

Regardless of my political views, I was raised to respect the President currently in office. As I am a conservative voice, I support President Trump. He has delivered results, and the economy is roaring. The black community was left behind in other administrations. There is record low unemployment.

Pastor Darrell Scott recently referred to him on Fox News as "the most pro-black president since the civil rights movement." I was raised to respect the flag and to stand for the National Anthem. I think that the removal of prayer in school has contributed to decline in culture. I suppose it's like the song, "anything goes." And so it goes.

The ultimate remedy is, of course, love and compassion. Is it so necessary to hurl expletives or perpetuate verbal attacks in person through intimidation because you are not in the same political party? The Congressional baseball practice shooting was done by a deranged male who had the names of Republican elected officials in his pocket. Racism and bigotry make no place in America. All hate groups like Neo-Nazi organizations and other extremists like white supremist groups must be condemned.

Majority Whip Steve Scalise of Louisiana was shot along with lobbyist Matt Mika. Two U.S. Capitol police officers were shot. Roger Williams - Texas, was injured while dodging bullets. He told me that all he could think about was an unborn grandchild that he wanted to live for.

I applaud human hurricane forces like Turning Point USA founder Charlie Kirk and Blexit founder Candace Owens. Both are forces to be reckoned with. They are targeting college and high school campuses and making it acceptable to be a conservative voice on campuses. TPUSA is promoting the values of free markets and small government. It's epic what Charlie and his organization have accomplished in 6 years.

While writing this book, I too, was tested. My apartment in a Manhattan high-rise went up in flames. Two-hundred firefighters were called to the scene. My neighbor died, and my clothing, furniture and cherished possessions were destroyed by flame, smoke and water damage.

When I went to visit the apartment, I was overcome with a smell so repulsive that I gagged. I quickly surmised that nothing could be saved. I left in tears. Walking through Central Park, I found the bench that the Mosbacher family had dedicated to my late husband, Bob. I sat on that bench at dusk and contemplated my life. It's what a friend and I like to call Park Bench Counseling. In my case, I was talking to God.

The disasters of 2017 were a reminder of many emotions of grief and strength. My home in Houston, Texas had suffered major losses during Hurricane Ike. Looking at the victims of Harvey, Irma, Maria, and Ophelia, I feel the pain of those who lost so much. **It's a leveling factor.** We all bleed the same, red blood. Everything can be erased in a second. All material things can be replaced. I think my life was transformed by the people I met writing this book. There is inherent goodness in people. **The H Factor.**

As Winston Churchill once said "When you are going through hell, just keep going." And storm survivors carried on. 2017 mass shootings and other acts of evil shuch as those in 2019 in El Paso, Texas and Dayton, Ohio do not define us. In the aftermath, communites united in prayer and banded together. They stayed strong despite adversity, grief and sorrow. Faith leaders comforted those who were reeling from shock and fear. *"Don't tell God how big your storm is. Tell the storm how big your God is."*

FOREWORD

Sutherland Springs:
A Texas Town in Mourning
Paul Buford - Pastor
November 2017

This has been a hard week for all of us in this community, state, country and even around the world. We have had an unprecedented tragedy take place here. Let me start out by saying, none of this took God by surprise.

Three weeks ago I said: We won't believe what God is about to do here in this church.

As far as this church, I believe that preparations for what has happened have been being put in place by God.

Did He cause this? No! Allow it? Yes! And so begins the questions. Why?

Let me also say, as Christians, we DO NOT believe that we are better than anyone else. But we DO believe that we have something of infinite value to share with others.

John 16:33, "In the world, you will have tribulation; but be of good cheer! I have overcome the world." NKN I John 5:4-5, "For whatever is born of God overcomes the world. And this is the victory that has overcome the world - our faith. 5 Who is he who overcomes the world, but he who believes that Jesus is the Son of God?" NKJV

Dealing with our grief.

John 11 :3-4

Therefore the sisters sent to Him, saying, "Lord, behold, he whom You love is

1 sick." 4 When Jesus heard that, He said, "This sickness is not unto death, but for the glory of God, that the Son of God may be glorified through it." NKJV

Mary rose up quickly and went out, followed her, saying, "She is going to the tomb to weep there."

32 Then, when Mary came where Jesus was, and saw Him, she fell down at His feet, saying to Him, "Lord, if You had been here, my brother would not have died." 33 Therefore, when Jesus saw her weeping, and the Jews who came with her ,veering. He groaned in the spirit and was troubled. 34 And He said, "Where have you laid him?"

They said to Him, "Lord, come and see." 35 Jesus wept. 36 Then the Jews said, "See how He loved him!"

37 And some of them said, "Could not this Man, who opened the eyes of the blind, also have kept this man from dying?" NKJV

If we continued to read, we would see that Lazarus is raised from the dead

1. We see at this point a lot of emotions and grief.

2. This is one of the greatest examples or pictures of the humanity of Christ.

3. Shows the compassion that He had.

4. It shows that He carried as a man the same emotions that we carry.

5. Vs. 35, Jesus wept - it means that He shed tears. When we see them talking of others weeping, it is a different word and it meant that they wailed or sobbed aloud.

6. Jesus performed many miracles. Did He know what God was about to do? We don't know, but we know for a fact that Jesus knew the power of God.

Third century Christian author/apologist Tertullian in his work Apologeticus wrote: "The blood of the martyrs is the seed of the church." With every drop that is spilled, many more are born. This is a direct relation to 'We will sow what we reap.' Every drop of blood of a reborn person can produce a crop of new born believers.

This was an evil act that took place.

Rom 12:17-21, Repay no one evil for evil. Have regard for good things in the sight of all men. 18 If it is possible, as much as depends on you, live peaceably with all men. 19 Beloved, do not avenge yourselves, but rather give place to wrath; for it is written, "Vengeance is Mine, I will repay," says the Lord. 20 If your enemy is hungry, feed him; If he is thirsty, give him a drink; For in so doing, you will heap coals of fire on his head. 21 **Do not be overcome by evil, but overcome evil with good." NKJV**

Do not be overcome by evil.

Overcome evil with good.

One evil act is now being encircled by and overcome by an exponentially greater amount of good.

All the good doesn't make the bad disappear, it doesn't remove it, but it overwhelms it and overcomes what it is that the evil thought that it would accomplish.

Our faith isn't shaken, it is strengthened.

There is a 100 year old tombstone in Indiana with this epitaph:

Pause stranger as you pass me by, As you are now, so once was I.

As I am now, so you will be, so prepare for death and follow me.

Someone scratched this last line:

To follow you I am not content, until I know which way you went.

Twenty six of our friends and family passed on at FBCSS last Sunday. I can tell you where those believers went.

John 14:6, Jesus said to him, "I am the way, the truth, and the life. No one comes to the Father except through Me." NKJV

I want everyone to think on this very hard. Where will you go when your day arrives? And what day will that be?

PART ONE

HURRICANE HARVEY TIMELINE

Sunday August 13, 2017
A tropical wave emerges off the West coast of Africa and merges with a low pressure area in Cabo Verde Islands.

Thursday, August 17, 2017
The National Hurricane Center identifies low pressure areas east of the Lesser Antilles and by 5 pm it is identified as Tropical Storm Harvey.

Friday, August 18, 2017
Tropical Storm Harvey passes over the Windward Islands with maximum sustained winds of 40 mph.

Saturday, August 19, 2017
Harvey weakens to a tropical depression, then becomes a wave.

Thursday, August 22, 2017
Remnants of Tropical Storm Harvey move across the Yucatan Peninsula.

Wednesday, August 23, 2017
Harvey regenerates into a tropical depression. A Hurricane Watch is issued north of Port Mansfield to San Luis Pass. Governor Greg Abbott declares a state of disaster for 40 Texas counties.

Thursday, August 24, 2017
Nueces County, Corpus Christi and Port Aransas issue mandatory evacuations. By noon, Harvey had strengthened to a Category 1 Hurricane and the NHC began predicting that it could be a Category 3 or higher.

Friday, August 25, 2017
At midnight, Harvey strengthened to a Category 2 and winds increased by morning to about 110 mph. Weather conditions on the coast began to deteriorate and outer rain-bands began sweeping across the lower and middle Texas coast.

By 2 pm, it was a Category 3 Hurricane. An EF0 tornado touched down 3 miles northeast of Seadrift. By 6 pm, it intensified to a Category 4 Hurricane. Harvey makes landfall on San Jose Island.

Saturday, August 26, 2017
Harvey makes second landfall on the northeastern shore of Copano Bay. Harvey is then downgraded to a Category 3.

Sunday, August 27, 2017
Harvey began moving slowly southeast toward Houston. Flooding emergencies began throughout the Houston area and the Southeastern Coast. Governor Abbott added 12 additional counties to his Presidential Disaster Declaration.

Monday, August 28, 2017
Harvey's center moved into the Gulf of Mexico with winds up to 45 mph. Catastrophic flooding continued in Southeastern Texas with tropical storms and storm surge warnings extended to Louisiana.

Tuesday, August 29, 2017
Rain and catastrophic flooding continued in southeastern Texas and into Louisiana. President Trump and Governor Abbott visit Corpus Christi and receive a detailed briefing.

TEXAS STRONG

"No force of nature is more powerful than Texans helping Texans, Americans helping Americans. In that generosity of spirit, Hurricane Harvey more than met its match. And we are grateful so many lives were spared."

"As we continue to rebuild following Hurricane Harvey's devastation across nearly 50,000 square miles of Texas - from our small coastal communities near Corpus Christi to Houston, Beaumont and beyond, I want to share my deep gratitude for all who came to our aid. In the moments of heroism and selflessness witnessed again and again since Harvey first made landfall that August night in 2017, and in the historic flooding that followed, we have seen the greatness of America. The armada of citizens and first responders who rushed to rescue those who could not save themselves reaffirms the value of every life and the unshakable bonds of our humanity. And the overwhelming outpouring of support, resources and prayers from individuals, churches, businesses, emergency responders and elected officials from around the country - and from leaders from around the world - has been truly inspiring."

"The damage from the storm was staggering even beyond its first landfall. But Texans have been challenged by disasters before. Whether hurricane, flood or fire, we have always come together and been made stronger. And though the road to recovery is still long as we rebuild homes, businesses and dreams, we will again triumph over tragedy - because when neighbors help neighbors, we all rise to higher ground."

- Governor Greg Abbott

1 HARVEY HITS TEXAS
"LIFTED UP THROUGH PRAYERS"

Hurricane Harvey began its assault on Texas on Friday, August 25th, 2017, causing massive destruction along the Coastal Bend before moving up the Texas coast into Central and Southeast Texas. An apocalyptic Category 4 storm, it raged into the Texas Coast between Port Aransas and Port O'Connor with unbridled wind speeds of 130 mph. Like a child having a temper tantrum, its rage was unrestrained, violent and unruly. Its mighty winds pummeled vulnerable homes and sturdy buildings. 42 foot utility poles became mere twigs in the hands of the wind.

Houston residents in the crosshairs of Harvey's aim, scrambled to shore up their homes and belongings. Mayor Turner was faced with a no win dilemma. Did he order an evacuation or not? If he did so, he would risk putting thousands of potentially stranded motorists in peril. A mass exodus might cause jammed exit routes and fuel shortages. Instead, he chose to issue evacuation orders for those areas most at risk. It was a good call.

Harvey wreaked havoc on sturdy trees, vehicles, solid businesses and homes. It mowed down everything in its pathway. A Niagara Fall-like rain was Harvey's constant companion. Like two tormented lovers having a very public tryst, the passionate cocktail of wind and rain showed no mercy. Its wild fury eased into Category 3 status but flood warnings were foreboding and ominous.

After dumping more than 43 inches of rain on August 29th, Texans began to wonder if the rain would ever stop. Where was Noah and his ark? By August 30th, it was downgraded to Tropical Storm Harvey but catastrophic life threatening floods continued. NOAA's National Hurricane Center warned that the flooding would continue into southeastern Texas and southwestern Louisiana.

More than 250,000 were without power already. Roads and interstates became waterways. People were stranded on roads and in their homes. As the water rose, roads became rivers. People were trapped in their neighborhoods as it creeped into houses, and residents faced a desperate waiting game. First responders and 911 call centers were stretched to their limit. Houston Mayor Sylvester Turner told residents that 911 operators would give preference to life threatening calls.

Houston Police advised residents to call other listed numbers for non-urgent requests. For those watching water rise into their homes, all requests for help seemed urgent. HPD was over-loaded and was also fielding calls regarding the status of roadways or weather. The U.S. Coast Guard was a collective army on steroids. The Coast Guard response included 2,600 active duty, reserve, civil and auxiliary personnel.

Their response included 50 fixed wing aircraft and 75 shallow water boats. Of those Coast Guard members living in Texas, several suffered catastrophic property damage themselves. Despite personal challenges, they focused on helping others. Residents with boats risked their own lives to help assist in the rescue effort. It was backbreaking labor and at times risky.

Governor Abbott enacted the Texas National Guard in response to the flooding. Millions were displaced and/or homeless. Houston's Barker Reservoir hit record levels as did the Addicks Reservoir. The Army Corps of Engineers was worried that the structures would breech. On Saturday, August 26th, Harris County officials began issuing warning of flooding in adjacent neighborhoods. Release of water was imminent.

Neighborhoods were already inundated and many inhabitants fled on foot. Others were rescued by boats or military vehicles. The city was in itself a swamp. On Tuesday, September 15th, Houston's NRG

Center, a massive 700,000 sq ft space, was converted into a primary mega shelter for the thousands of evacuees. County Judge Ed Emmett announced that the shelter would be run by a local nonprofit, Baker-Ripley and CEO Angela Blanchard. Along with help from FEMA, the center would include a pharmacy, children's center, medical treatment area and quarters for showering and sleeping and eating. A designated area for pets, in cooperation with Houston's animal shelter, was established.

Heading up the enormous efforts was former Harris County Judge, Robert Eckels and former Houston Mayor Annise Parker. The cavernous space could accommodate 10,000 people and also a variety of representatives from various social services. A city within a city had been created in 24 hours.

A call went out for volunteers on social media. They were instructed to bring identification and to check-in at Entrance 10. They came in droves. By 10pm, when the first Metro buses pulled into the parking lot, they were ready. There were about 1,000 dazed and displaced residents at the shelter by Wednesday morning.

A second mega shelter was operated by the American Red Cross. It was located at the George R. Brown Convention Center downtown. Gail McGovern, president and CEO, issued a press statement on September 1st, stating, "Last night, more than 42,000 people sought refuge in 258 Red Cross and partner's shelters across Texas, with 1500 staying in six emergency shelters in Louisiana." She continued, "Donations pay to transport 2,300 disaster workers to Texas and pay for the cots, blankets and hygiene kits as well as the 392,000 meals and snacks we and partners have served since the storm began."

The Salvation Army deployed 78 mobile feeding units to Texas. Disaster workers were mobilized from all over the United States and Canada. The Area Command relocated to Dallas and five incident command teams coordinated service delivery and assistance to Beaumont, Corpus Christi and other affected areas. They were supporting one of the largest relief efforts in history. Their motto is "Doing the Most Good," and that certainly rang true during their monumental task.

Governor Abbott issued a proclamation stating, in part," Texans have remained strong throughout this ordeal with neighbor by neighbor wading into the flood waters or sorting through wind damage to rescue fellow residents. The people of Texas are grateful for the outpouring of support and resources from around the country and around the world that have been sent to Texas to assist with the damage as we begin the process of healing and rebuilding. Throughout our history, Texans have been strengthened, assured and lifted up through prayer."

The Proclamation continued to declare Sunday, September 3rd, 2017, as a Day of Prayer in Texas. The Governor urged Texans of all faiths and religious traditions and backgrounds to offer prayers on that day for the safety of first responders, public safety officers, and military personnel, healing of individuals, rebuilding communities and the restoration of the entire region struck by this disaster."

In the aftermath, legions of not for profits and citizens in virtually every state reached out to help. Houston civic leaders swung into action to lend a hand. Restaurant owners supplied free meals and businesses donated essential supplies. Celebrities established GoFundMe pages and planned fundraisers.

One of Houston's most famous athletes stepped up to help. Houston Texan's JJ Watt announced he was fundraising and raised $4.6 million dollars. Quarterback Tom Brady and Bill Belichick gave $100,000 and $50,000 respectively. Watt's response was, "It's incredibly kind gestures. Just goes to show what kind of people they are, despite everything- playing a game against each other, having practice against each other, and being in the same conference with each other and things like that. For them to step up in a time like this and just help their fellow humans is pretty special and I think it speaks volumes to their characters." Once again, that's the **Hurricane Factor** at work.

UFC's Heavyweight Champ Derrick Lewis "the Black Beast," rescued children from flood waters. He was the definition of a true champion in every way.

Federal, statewide and local officials worked seamlessly in their tireless response efforts. The Texas delegation put aside politics and worked together to help their constituents. Senators Cornyn, McCaul and Senator Cruz along with representatives like Sheila Jackson Lee helped those feeling the brunt of Harvey. Lee was a tireless advocate for her inner-city constituency that was hit hard.

In fact, the whole downtown theatre district was devastated by Harvey from the storm's first act to its final curtain call.

Federal agencies coordinated in lockstep and FEMA representatives were dispatched immediately. The recovery and rebuilding process would be costly and long but the can do of Texas Strong residents was evident every step of the way. Governor Abbott was praised for his leadership and response and was a steadying force throughout the ensuing aftermath.

At times, gas lines resembled the endless sea of people at a Trump rally. Many waited tirelessly for hours in line. Once it was their turn, they were disappointed to find out that fuel- the star attraction- was MIA. Hotel rooms were overbooked and nerves were frayed. Still there were examples of beautiful, kind spirits everywhere. These souls are what I like to call light bearers. "Do unto others," the Golden Rule was personified in Harvey's aftermath. Generosity became a state of being.

It's been said that greatness is a choice in the moment. Those Hurricane Harvey moments afforded many the opportunity to step up and do the right thing. It was overwhelming to witness others lighting candles in a dark room. The storm brought out the best in others and this **factor** was a major consolation prize. In the fragile moments when people are scared and lonely, they were not abandoned.

2 THE TRUMP FACTOR

President Trump and his new administration was put to the ultimate test when Harvey hit. Harvey became the most destructive storm since Katrina. NOAH'S office of Coastal Management estimated that Harvey's price tag would be $125 billion - making it the costliest storm in history. At least 47 deaths were reported and 100,000 homes damaged or destroyed.

President Trump was fully engaged from the outset of the ominous forecasts by the National Hurricane Center and reassured those residents in harm's way that they would not be forgotten. And they were not.

From day 1, President Trump's excellent crisis management skills were evident. After the storm pummeled the Texas coast, he first visited Rockport. His first stop was at First Baptist Church where he was joined by evangelical pastor Franklin Graham.

He then continued to Corpus Christi with his wife, Melania, and was joined by Governor Greg Abbott and cabinet secretaries and federal and state leaders. He said, "This storm was of epic proportion. Nobody's ever seen anything like this and I just want to say that working with Texas Governor Greg Abbott and his entire team has been an honor."

He later added, "Texas can handle anything." The crowd cheered as he said, "We love you." Vice President Pence came a short while later. "There is no storm as tough as Texas," Gov. Abbott said when he introduced Vice President Pence. In his words, warm and measured, Pence reassured Texans that President Trump wanted its citizens to know that the "full resources of the national government are being brought to bear in a consistent way." He later went to work at a nearby young couple's home and helped drag fallen tree branches off of the front lawn.

FEMA (Federal Emergency Management Agency) Administrator William Brock Long reassured reporters that more than 21,000 federal workers had been dispatched for the response effort. Recovery would be a tall order but FEMA, the Coast Guard, National Guard, Army Corps of Engineers and other agencies were up to the task.

President Trump immediately pushed for $7.85 billion in Federal funding and emergency relief spending. He also made a second trip to Texas where he and the First Lady Melania visited the NRG Center one of two large downtown shelters. He engaged with those most impacted by the hurricane and helped to serve meals and reassured distraught and displaced citizens. The First Couple announced a donation of $1 million for relief - with $300,000 going to the Red Cross and the balance to other agencies.

He later spoke at First Church in Pearland, Texas, along with Governor Abbott and Senator Ted Cruz. In Houston, Mayor Turner did an excellent job with coordination of first responders and the multiple city offices under his purview. In fact, when the going gets tough, the tough got going, including state senators like John Cornyn and representative Sheila Jackson Lee and the entire Texas delegation. City officials coordinated their efforts in lockstep.

Remarkably, Democrats and Republicans united and worked in concert. While this camaraderie is not always on display in Congress, the crisis factor brought out the best in lawmakers. This unity in crisis is the true "**Hurricane Factor.**" If only our nation could dispense with such hostility when others disagree.

As President Trump remarked, "There is no rest for the weary." His words rang true when Hurricane Irma pounded Florida in September. It was the strongest storm observed in the Atlantic in terms of maximum sustained winds since Wilma. It was also the first Category 5 storm to hit the Leeward Islands on record.

There were 52 direct fatalities, and it became the fifth costliest cyclone on record with an estimated $64.76 billion in property damage. Governor Rick Scott, Ron Desantis, and the Florida delegation worked tirelessly to restore some semblance of normalcy to Florida. Again, state, local and federal officials collaborated to restore power- 60,000 plus workers were working around the clock.

President Trump visited Ft. Meyers, Florida on September 14th and handed out hoagie sandwiches in the storm battered state. Thousands of homes were without electricity and residents were shell shocked. President Trump considers Florida his second home, and he reassured residents that the Federal government would not let them down. "We have been very, very fast, and we had to be," he said. "We were signing papers as the storm came in."

On Irma's heels, Maria came along and was regarded to be the worst natural disaster on record to affect Dominica and Puerto Rico. Winds were clocked at 155 mph. Hundreds of Puerto Rico's 3.4 million residents were without electricity and drinking water. The infrastructure was already failing when the storm hit and so recovery would be very slow.

The island was in dire economic straits already, and migration to the U.S. Mainland in 2014 was at historically high levels. The Commonwealth's Institute of Statistics revealed that 84,000 people, or 2% of its population, immigrated to the U.S. due to the economy.

Asked by reporters how he would rate the federal government's response, Trump declared, "I give ourselves a 10."

First responders were spread razor thin. Still, Puerto Rican governor, Ricardo Rossello, while at the White House in late October, told President Trump that he did "a great job." He added, "you responded immediately sir… but there's a lot left to do."

Some argue with FEMA's results but it's been acknowledged that rebuilding would be an ongoing slow process through 2018.

Nevertheless, President Trump weathered these three natural disasters with flying colors.

3 BEAUTY IN
THE SUFFERING

L ike so many fellow Houstonians, Aric Harding and his wife Glenna, were focused on shoring up their home in Friendswood. A snug neighborhood with a population of over 35,000, it was a bustling kid-friendly area with superior schools and safe places to play. Aric's home was not in a mandatory evacuation zone, and he had an oversupplied pantry and a well built modern dwelling. His household was as unpredictable as the Hurricane. Harding was blessed with 5 boys and 2 girls ranging in ages 5 to 13: Rylor, Everett, Harper, Monroe, Jasper, Aliza and Judah. The Hardings also had an inside dog named Rosie. Although things did not seem so rosy on that fateful evening.

A worship leader at the Clear Creek Community Church and part time musician, Aric is a man of deep spirituality. He relied on God for guidance in his everyday life and trusted Him for protection and strength in times of testing of faith. He sought to reassure his wife and children once the rain began on Saturday. As they hunkered down, it pounded their roof like a jackhammer. After spending a largely sleepless night, checking outside and looking for leaks, daylight winked at him. It was about mid-morning Saturday when he was confronted with the terrible realization that the street was becoming a river and that water was steadily enveloping his front yard.

As Aric looked outside in horror he began having a conversation with God. "I wrestled with God and the decision to stay or go."

Asking God for advice, Aric prayed out loud, "Please don't let me be the victim. I need your advice. Hear me out God. What do I do?"

At that point, it was crystal clear that there was no safe exit from the house for the family. Swimming in uncharted stormwater was not a good choice. There was a very clear and present danger, and he was running out of options. He felt lost.

He began praying, "I am exhausted and flood weary. I trust your judgement." He then knew what to do. "Alright, you are in charge. I will go and wake up my family." He obediently and reluctantly woke up his wife and sleepy children. Glenna looked around at her home, which was her sanctuary and refuge. She home-schooled the children, and all the happy, cherished belongings of a well-lived safe harbor were everywhere.

Aric, however, had another insurmountable obstacle. He needed a way out. The last hour became his finest hour because he looked out and there was a canoe making a slow steady cruise down the street. "He just showed up. It turned out that it was this guy from our church, paddling down the flooded streets to see who needed rescuing." God had heard his fervent prayers.

He managed to load all the kids and the dog into the canoe. "We traveled down a few streets and some neighbors we had never met, Charlie and Mary Taylor, took us in," he recalled. "They were so kind. To think they even had a dog who later became best pals with Rosie."

He learned the valuable lesson of being a happy recipient of help when it's offered. "I have often found many ways to serve but being served is humbling for me. I had to learn to receive and learn to be helped. He also learned humility and to swallow his pride. "One day I am going to take a step back and go, 'Alright God, you know better!' It's hard to accept help but being served is a different kind of power."

After a few days, Aric, along with a friend, was able to wade back to his house and bring back things that were important to his kids to their new temporary home. "I grabbed a trash bag and loaded it with provisions and gathered up teddy bears, stuffed animals and video games- anything the kids could hold onto," said Aric. As he splashed through ankle to waist high water in his living room, he tried not to take in the heart wrenching water damage.

"Rylor is a naturally gifted musician and piano player who has won many competitions. Standing in the living room in the middle of a lake was his piano. Since I couldn't pack it up, I decided to play it and have John take a video so that I could show Rylor that it was okay."

"I sat down, and I just started noodling...playing anything that came into my head. I am a guitar player, not a pianist, and I knew Rylor would make fun of me regardless of what I played," he reminisced.

His video went viral. "We posted that video online and social media played it far and wide. Music at the right moment can give people a sense of an event - it can encapsulate a moment in time in the right way."

For Aric, the hardest part was seeing all of his soggy possessions and the precious memories they represented. "We have flood insurance as our mortgage required it, so we will be alright," he stated. "I hope my kids look back on this experience and remember what God did in our lives as it was a turning point."

At the printing of this book, the Hardings were back in their home and are the owners of a brand new Yamaha piano, compliments of Grammy-nominated singer-songwriter Vanessa Carlton, who saw the video online. "Sometimes music is the only thing that gets you through," she tweeted.

RIC SALVIDAR
"In my Prayers"

Ricardo (Ric) Salvidar lives in a modest neighborhood in Northwest Houston. His family endured a tragedy that caught international attention. His brother Sammy, drove a van through an unpredictable and unnavigable roadway of high water on Greens River Drive. His passengers, that included his parents Manuel Salvidar, age 84, wife Belia, age 81, and their four grandchildren, Devy, 16, Dominic, 14, Xavier, 8, and Daisy, 6, died in a terrible accident. Desperate to get to higher ground, he had attempted to cross the bridge over Green's Bayou.

Tragically, the van was carried away by the current. Sammy had cracked the driver's side window to gauge the water level and was able to escape. He desperately clung to a tree branch for about 45 minutes until help finally arrived.

"It was a miracle the driver was rescued," said Harris County Sheriff Ed Gonzalez. "Unfortunately, the rest of the family drowned." It took three days before the waters receded and the submerged van was located.

Ric said that Sammy faced an insurmountable amount of of guilt. "I don't blame Sammy for the accident," he stressed. He said that they both miss their parents and that the whole family was reeling from the blow. "They were scheduled to celebrate their 60th wedding anniversary in October."

Both elder Salvidars were Alzheimer patients and Sammy had been asked that fateful day by brother, Danny, to get the keys to the van and pick up their parents and the great-grandchildren and bring them to Ric's house. He had hesitated when he came to the bridge but apparently his father had told him to forge ahead so he followed orders.

Due to the churning water, it was impossible for Sammy to rescue his family trapped inside the submerged van. He barely got out, screaming and screaming for help. "Sammy told me that mom was looking at dad when the water rushed into the van and that dad did not look scared," Ric explained. "We find it comforting that they were together."

Ric had trouble sleeping. He watched tv and often thought of his parents late at night, remembering the stories they told him growing up. "Dad's favorite saying was 'There is more than one way to skin a cat' -He always said there was always a way to get things done and he did not want to hear there was no way to fix things."

He witnessed an outpouring of help from neighbors and people who had worked with his dad who was a diesel mechanic and an Air Force veteran. They received so much food that he invited other relatives to eat it. "While we were at mom's and dad's that week, people drove by and gave us sandwiches, water, hot dogs, hamburgers... one guy drove by asking if we needed toilet paper," he said.

He found that the best part of the hurricane was how strangers helped other strangers. "It did not matter what age or creed or race or religion- people were there to help," he reflected. He met so many wonderful people who helped with the general chores at his parent's home. "More hands reaching out offering instead of reaching out wanting something."

Ric considers himself a man of faith and said that prayers had sustained him during his lowest moments. "I miss them so much but God is helping me out because of my prayers," he said. "It helped when people said to me, 'You are in my prayers.' "

The Salvidars were buried at Brookside Memorial Park in northwest Houston. While it was a sad day, the family focused on their parents' incredible love story. "Where one went, the other went," he stated.

Belia and Manuel met when she was a carhop in Corpus Christi, and he was stationed at the nearby air force base. They were married 59 years and three days. After the waterlogged van was discovered, they were holding hands in the front seat.

"I often prayed that my parents would die at the same time," he reminisced.

Virginia Salvidar also echoed his sentiment. "They all went together and we take comfort in that."

For Mona Salvidar, a dental assistant, who lost her four children, it will also be a long road back from grief. On Saturday, September 2nd, a fundraiser was held at the Principe de Paz Pentecostal Church that was overflowing with family and friends including classmates in the Pasadena Independent School District. It was an emotionally charged day with many attendees choking up. Generosity poured in following the tragedy as the community chipped in to defray funeral costs and a GoFundMe account was established.

On Monday, the day of the funeral, the church was once again crowded with those wishing to comfort and pay respect to the family. The children's father, Jason Salvidar, expressed his heartbreak. He said that they also take comfort in the fact that the children died together.

The Salvidar tragedy touched the collective hearts of the nation including deceased superstar Selena's father, Abraham Quintanilla, who is related to the Salvidars. In a facebook post, he said, "Manuel's mother was my father's first cousin. My condolences to the family."

Ric said Abraham reached out to him directly and offered to help. "Despite all the bad news, there was so much good news right in the middle of the suffering," he recalled.

4 HARVEY'S
FIRST RESPONDERS

"DOING SOMETHING DIFFERENT EVERYDAY IS THE JOY OF BEING A POLICE OFFICER."
-HPD NORBERT RAYMOND

Houston Police Officer Norbert Ramon saved approximately 1,500 lives during Hurricane Harvey despite a diagnosis of Stage 4 cancer. A 24-year veteran of the department, Norbert, 55, was diagnosed with colon cancer during a routine colonoscopy about 18 months ago, and doctors told him that he might have six to eight years to live.

For this Houston strong responder, illness doesn't slow him down. "I don't want to dwell on my illness," he firmly stated. "My wife Cindy knows what to expect. I just want to be treated as normal."

This is Officer Norbert's story.

***

On Saturday, August 27th, his day was anything but normal. "It was raining pretty heavy, and I was on the Eastex freeway," he recalled. "Cars were coming northbound at me and the freeway was flooded so they were coming back the opposite way and turning around," he recalled.

"There was an officer directing them off the freeway. I'm in uniform- so I took an exit and started heading back towards my house in Huffman," he added. He then called his supervisor for instructions.

"If we can't make it to a station, when you can't reach your designated one, you go to the nearest one," he explained.

"I am assigned to the Traffic Enforcement division downtown, but I couldn't get there when the flash floods began. Following department protocol, Ramon instead responded to the closest duty station, which was HPD's Lake Patrol Unit on Lake Houston near Atascocita."

Between Sunday, August 27th, and Tuesday, August 29th, Ramon and other officers used four police boats to move more than 1,500 Houstonians out of the flash floods that submerged neighborhoods near Interstate 10 and Federal Road, along with subdivisions in Kingwood.

"I went to Lake Patrol - Sgt. in Charge, Epi Garza, who knows my health situation, (the other guys didn't know), I just said, 'let me go - count me in,' " he said.

He didn't want to be treated any differently. "I just want to be one of the guys."

"We went to location Federal and Normandy, a bunch of apartment residences next to a bayou with 6 ft or 7 ft of water. We had taken boats from Lake Patrol there. We found a way to unload them, rolling them back to float. From that point on it was just a ferry, we would go to the apartments full of water. All the bottom floor apartments were full of water. They would hand me children from the balcony - I would carry them in my arms to the boat," he recalled.

"No one I rescued knew about my illness but I was quite comfortable. The police guys gave me a jacket with a life jacket built in it. It's a Houston Police Dept. one. I got soaked and never got cold," he added.

He and his team rescued people in dire circumstances for 8+ hours. "We had to stop before dark so we could get back to our station," he said. "We stayed overnight at the station."

The next morning, Monday, August 28th, the team moved all the equipment out of the police station, Lake Patrol, as the water was rising into the bottom level of the station.

"The following day, we went to Kingwood. The current was treacherous, it was so strong. It threw 6 officers into the water. They were rescued by other responders as they had life jackets on," he stated.

"I was in a different boat. As the current was swift, I put another life jacket on over my first jacket." Conditions were less than ideal.

They even rescued officers at Kingwood police station. "We had to be careful of the power lines. Once we got back to a safe area, we were notified that there was volunteer help coming."

"We had to fix the bilge pump in our boat before we could go further. Once we got it repaired, we were sent to rescue senior citizens. Houston Police Dive Team were also there pulling people out," he added. The elderly folks they rescued were grateful.

"They were very calm. The dive team picked them up in their wheelchairs in our boats to take them somewhere safe. They were concerned about their pets and medicine," said Ramon, "but relieved to be out of harm's way."

"They were in great spirit. We told them that they were on a cruise," he laughed.

Ramon and his team rescued people for hours. "They all wanted to know where they were going. We were taking them to shelters," he recalled.

Although they primarily rescued people on ground floors, some even debated whether to come with them. "We had to coax them to leave."

"They'd have the kids in blankets and stuff. I'm picking them up and putting them in the boat, trying to put their umbrellas on. My partner was trying to drive the boat. He's got all these umbrellas blocking his view of the water," he laughed. The effort wasn't his first crisis.

"This isn't the first hurricane. I have worked in Katrina and Rita - not my first rodeo," he said.

Ramon's optimistic spirit and profound faith kept him going. "When I wake up, I go to my truck, kneel down, look up at the sky, and say to God, ' thank you for today and allow me to go to work and be healthy today,' " he added.

"My main concern was to help the citizens. Nothing else was on my mind. I didn't worry about me or anything." The extreme conditions could have cost many their lives .

"It was desperate. I mean you've never seen so much water before."

His quiet strength and his resolve strengthened when he was diagnosed with cancer, his unwavering joy comes from faith. "I remember being diagnosed with cancer March 2016- (when I was 50, I was told I had polyps)," he said. "I woke up from the colposcopy. I'm half dazed. The doctors say 'you have cancer- go get a scan, do this, do that.' "

He was diagnosed with stage four colon cancer which since has spread to his liver and lungs.

"That revelation came 18 months ago. At the time, doctors told me I might have six to eight years to live."

"We all gotta go sometime. I don't want to have a time stamp on me."

After three days on a rescue boat during Hurricane Harvey, Ramon drove eight hours to the Cancer Treatment Centers of America clinic in Tulsa for chemotherapy. "I usually fly to Oklahoma but Houston's two airports were closed." His attitude is inspirational to all who are going through this health challenge.

"I asked the Lord 'why me' and then said 'why not me - look at my position, where I'm at, the Lord can use me as a messenger. I'm a police officer, I'm always in the public eye to tell other people and to spread the Word."

After the storm, the hospital staff saw the photos posted of his rescue work and contacted him. He is not just a patient. They cared.

"They were worried about my health and reached out to me. 'Hey, how are you guys doing? - We're seeing all the photos and wanted to check up on you.' "

"It's been an emotional roller coaster, and they believe I am a hero," he recalled modestly. And he and other dedicated officers deserve a parade in their honor.

Officer Ramon continues to get chemotherapy every two week and to work a full 40 hr week. "I'm a traffic enforcement officer- I monitor speeds, look for DUI's and other aggressive drivers," he explained. The job isn't easy, but he stays focused on service to others.

His message to other cancer patients is to not get down. "Just continue to plug away and be happy," he said. "Don't let cancer consume your life."

Officer Ramon passed away in June 2018 -just before publication. He was laid to rest in San Antonio and recognized for his unselfish acts of courage and concern for others.

THE KEN SUTCLIFFE STORY: TEXAS TASK FORCE II

"TEXANS RESPOND DRAMATICALLY"

Ken Sutcliffe is a 30-year veteran with the Texas Fire Department Task Force II (TX-TF2) at one of the 28 federal teams under FEMA Urban Search and Rescue system. From August 24th through September 15th, Sutcliffe was assigned to the ESF 9 Desk, whose mission is to provide search and rescue coordination and support services for emergency events in Texas during disaster. The ESF 9 resources are used when individual agencies are overwhelmed and county emergency requests additional fire/search and rescue assistance.

Texas Task Force II went operational in 2007 to respond to human-caused or natural disasters in the state. After Dallas Fire Rescue proposed a search-and-rescue team that could complement the existing Texas Task Force I, a 70-member squad funded by the Federal Emergency Management Agency (FEMA) that responds to disasters country wide was established.

Ken's wife Andrea (Andi) is a Member Relations Coordinator with Texas Task Force II and a Disaster Canine Handler. Skye, a border collie, was paired with Andi in 2013, and they achieved their basic Type 11 State Urban Search and Rescue Alliance (SUSAR) certification and their advanced certification in record time. In May of 2015, they went on their first deployment when a tornado touched down in Runaway Bay, Texas. Skye dug through the debris of a collapsed building and confirmed that no humans were trapped in the wreckage.

Andi suffers from hypogammaglobulinemia which is a type of immunodeficiency disease that impairs the immune system. It is managed with plasma infusions every four weeks. When Skye is not on active duty, he also doubles as a therapy dog for others receiving treatment at the facility where she is a patient.

Ken Sutcliffe has been married to Andrea since Sept 4th, 2011, and celebrated their 6th anniversary during Hurricane Harvey. His selflessness is an inspiration.

This is Ken Sutcliffe's story.

***

"We were deployed during our anniversary. I was in the State Operations Center (SOC), Austin, Texas - where all the ESF Emergency Service Functions gather," he explained.

The State of Texas Emergency Manager decides when he deploys. "It always depends on the level of a threat: hurricanes, large tornados, heavy flooding, etc."

"I have been a fireman for over 30 years," he said. "I am the luckiest guy. I wanted to be a fireman and be in the army and got to do both."

Ken was with the 2nd Army Cavalry Regiment in Germany 1980 -1984. "This was pre-satellite/drone days, and you physically had to scout the enemy," he said. "I patrolled the Czech - German border."

He started firefighting in 1987 when he moved from California to Texas.

His first job in 1988 was at Oakcliff Texas Fire Station No 23. "We had the old pole that you had to slide down, but they got rid of it as too many injured ankles. One night, I fell into the pole hole and got injured," he laughed.

The SOC is different. "It functions as a 24 hour monitoring response center." They worked 24 hour shifts and then got 48 hours off.

"In State Operations Centre, we have to think strategically," he explained. "We had to see where resources were going to be needed, what's going to be happening 24/7 hours ahead, and so I worked the night shift from 7pm to 7am," he added.

It was his job to coordinate Emergency Services Function 9 work. "I worked the search and rescue desk that determined if there were any search and rescue assets- helicopters, fixed wing craft, boats, all the type used for urban search and rescue task forces - a 70 person team that can be self sufficient for 72 hrs."

During Hurricane Harvey, he started August 24th and came home Sept 15th. Those were grueling long hours even for veterans like himself. People's lives were on the line and there was no luxury of time for personal lives. Ken's main focus was those under his watch.

"At night, any kind of request for any emergency search and rescue asset I controlled," he said. "I knew when I came on duty how many boats we had and what our plans were."

"I had an outlay of anything we had," he added.

If there were requests, he would contact local emergency centers and allocate assets to them. "My job specifically was to make sure a team doing the search and rescue had the the assets they needed," said Ken.

"For Hurricane Harvey Urban Search Rescue Task Force 2, the Federal Gov. sent six Type 1 Task Forces like teams. We had eight Type 1 search and rescue task forces, six Type 3 Urban Search and Rescue Task Forces, fourteen Mission Ready Packaged Water, two boat squads and extra personnel."

"FEMA stripped the other water assets from other teams and sent them to us."

They rescued 24,000 to 26,000 people in task forces that were a combination of firefighters (fifteen Dallas-area fire stations provided volunteers), structural engineers, doctors, canine handlers and tech specialists.'

"There were moments - I was concerned -when 911 was overloaded, and we tried to move as many assets into Houston when it was storming severely," he recollected.

"When winds reach 60 mph, we can't put rescuers out, which is why Governor Greg Abbott warned people to evacuate early in the day, preceding Hurricane Harvey." At a certain point, people ignoring evacuation orders would be on their own. Texas as a whole is a state where people live in separate neighborhoods. But any time there is a disaster, Texans respond dramatically to help others," he said.

"Texas is a state where people try to help others. A lot of this is going back to the time, Texas was its own country, being independent and different."

Hurricanes are logistically the most challenging. "There's such a wide area of damage - tens of square miles of devastation - requiring vast amounts of manpower to search. It's an exhaustive process and requires highly skilled manpower."

"We felt like threats within the North Texas area - due to the weather and otherwise - specifically required that this region have its own response team that could respond quicker," said Ken.

Texas Task Force II, meanwhile, has been deployed seven times since its formation 10 years ago, including to hurricanes Ike and Gustav, the West explosion and the Granbury tornado that devastated parts of Hood County in May 2013. There were six fatalities and $272 million in damages in that disaster alone.

He also worked during Hurricane Ike and the West Texas Fertilizer explosion in 2013. 15 people were killed, 160 were injured and 150 buildings were damaged. The cause was arson.

ANDI'S ROLE

It was a love story meant to be. "I could not be prouder of anything in my life than Andrea."

"My mother was living in Dallas area, and I would become more and more comfortable every time I was there." There he met the love of his life.

"I met Andrea (Andi) in Dallas. She was looking for help to move, and she knew guys at EMT that helped people move. I volunteered to help her move with some other guys." The rest is history. "From that point, I was smitten," he smiled. "I would send her flowers at work and say that I was patiently waiting. We had our first date in 2008 when we went to a Stars hockey game," he said.

Texas Task Force II currently has 6 dogs with handlers, like Skye. All are taught to find survivors. None are known as "cadaver dogs." The dogs are incredible at what they do," he said.

The dogs go into areas where they can't send rescue technicians-areas with a great deal of dangerous potential for collapsing buildings and such.

"They can smell things we can't even begin to get close to. It's a scent. We have high-tech listening devices, fiber optic cameras, but none matches the capability of a well-trained canine to make live finds. They're truly amazing," he stated.

"When our task force was looking for canine handlers, I knew Andrea would like to do it," he added. "She applied but didn't want me to help her out. She wanted to do it on her own. That's how it started."

Ken, like every doting husband, worried about his wife. "I could not say I never thought about Andrea's task force not going. During Hurricane Harvey, of course I was concerned - she knows there is job to be done and does not flinch. She has a tremendous work ethic and is great at what she does."

His favorite saying is from Edmund Burke: "the only necessity for evil to triumph is for good men to do nothing."

Edmund Burke was an Irish statesman born in Dublin, as well as an author, orator, political theorist, and philosopher who, after moving to London, served as a member of parliament for many years in the House of Commons with the Whig Party. Ken identifies with Burke's strong work ethic and words of wisdom as does Andi.

Neither Andi or Ken think too much about retirement. "I have been in the fire service 30 years. I would hate to leave. I know the day is coming. I figured 3 more years and then maybe I'll retire," he said.

"I will always work for the state, teach part-time at Texas A and M University- the engineers' extension branch that has a free school and disaster training. I would teach wide area searching and search and rescue in community disaster," he stated. Meanwhile he is honored to serve.

Andi and Skye have no immediate plans except to continue to work. "We have 3 other dogs," Ken said. Beau is a rescue dog and a tripod dog who has 3 legs. "Sadly they think when they found him he was used as bait for fighting dogs. We found him through Operation Kindness," he explained. "He looks like Scooby-Doo."

The third is Brindy, "a black mouth Cur and boxer mix - a kinda genetic hound dog from the Florida - Georgia area. Andrea found her and all the dogs get along fine."

Like Skye, the dogs form special camaraderies with their first responders and Texas is lucky to have such amazing partnerships and all creatures great and small.

5 TEXAS STATE GUARD TO THE RESCUE

"EQUAL TO THE TASK"

Founded in 1871, the Texas State Guard (TXSG), is one of three branches of the Texas Military and under command of the Governor of Texas.

The mission of the TXSG is to provide mission-ready military forces to assist in times of state emergencies including hurricanes.

Geoffrey (Geoff) Connor, LCDR, is an attorney, former Secretary of State, and historian with a long history of public service in Texas. He was deployed to Houston in Operation Harvey at the Command Center established at Katy High School.

This is Geoff's story in his own words.

***

Geoff has the rank of Lieutenant Commander (LCDR) in the Texas State Guard. "I am assigned as a JAG officer (legal officer) to the Texas Maritime Regiment (TMAR). After Hurricane Harvey, I received orders first to Camp Mabry headquarters and was subsequently deployed to Houston in Operation Harvey. I was at the Command Center established at Katy High School," he said.

Although normally performing only legal duties as a JAG, all TMAR officers are trained in boat operations, search and rescue, and water rescue. "Because of the great need in the field, I was deployed for boat operations in the Memorial neighborhood. We operated with one TMAR member and one DPS trooper to each boat, typically 14-18 foot civilian boats, where we could carry people and sometimes pets from their homes to safety. We also carried food, water, and medical supplies," said Connor.

Some people rescued from their homes had initially refused assistance because they believed the water would quickly recede, and they wanted to stay to protect their property. However, after a few days with the release of water from Addicks Reservoir, some people changed their minds and wanted to leave.

"During the time we were living at Katy High School, we had food and supplies transported to us by the military. However, we had huge donations by local citizens to include food, bedding, toiletries, towels, suntan lotion, bug spray, and whatever they thought we could use," he said.

They would arrive back at the campus soaked, muddy and filthy from the flooded conditions. The athletic staff and parents of Katy High School athletes organized themselves into 24 hour teams of people to wash, dry and fold clothes and towels.

"We could drop our clothes when headed to the locker room showers, and the next day it would be in folded stacks along the hallway for us to pick up. (Our military uniforms and gear have our names on them, so they could separate it and we could easily find our belongings). People brought a hundred boxes of Shipley donuts, a hundred Domino pizzas, cases of bottled water or anything they thought would make us feel supported, appreciated and loved. It was a great bonding experience among the troops deployed and between us and the communities we served."

Hurricane Harvey had a devastating impact on Houston and the region. However, Houston has survived other disasters over its history since its founding in 1836. It has the great human capacity to handle serious blows, recover and rebound to new heights. "Houston is not just a great Texas city, it is one of the great cities of the world," he said.

6 HOLY RESPONDER

"MY TEMPLE WILL BE CALLED A HOUSE OF PRAYER FOR PEOPLE OF ALL NATIONS" ISAIAH 56:7

Father David Bergeron of the Catholic Charismatic Center in Houston was returning home from his brother Francois' home after watching the Mayweather v McGregor fight on Saturday night and ended up stuck in the storm and sleeping in his truck on an overpass.

On Sunday morning, he woke up to administer Catholic mass. His makeshift setting was atypical. He used a kayak to travel to stranded parishioners and bless them.

Founded in Houston in 1972, the Catholic Charismatic Center - a spirituality grounded in the charismatic movement that has congregation-lively liturgies with upbeat music. Its congregation is roughly 80 percent Hispanic.

Staffed since 1999 by members of the Companions of the Cross religious order to which Bergeron belongs, the Center is located in downtown Houston.

Launched in 1985 in Ottawa, Canada by a priest involved in the charismatic movement named father Bob Bedard, the Companions of the Cross now include roughly forty priests as well as a related community of sisters and a body of lay associates. Bishop Christian Riesbeck, an auxiliary bishop of Ottawa and the Vicar General of the archdiocese, is also a member of the Companions of the Cross, as is Bishop Scott McGaig of Canada's military ordinariate.

This is Father Bergeron's story in his words.

***

"The storm was starting on Saturday night," he recalled, "and I was receiving text messages about the weather and tornado warnings on my phone but I was driving." He was trying to make it back to his brother's home, which was only about five miles away. "I got another text when I was three miles away---it was a powerless situation." He had to pull over and spend a miserable night in his truck.

"As it was Sunday morning, I woke up ready to do what every priest does that day, which is to say Sunday Mass." An avid kayaker, he journeyed to the Charismatic Center by kayak. He had seen several people who were stranded so he kayaked to a convenience store to buy food to give away to those in need.

"I tried to buy wine for communion but there is a ban in Texas regarding buying wine before noon so I had to rely on my faith." With a keen sense of humor, he quipped "I have faith but I didn't have enough faith to perform water into wine like JESUS did."

Father Bergeron bought his supplies and returned by kayak, to the same street where he had passed people stranded on the second floor of an apartment building. "One man was trying to cross the street that was now covered in several feet of water, and I thought it was too dangerous to cross so I escorted him over to his son."

While praying to God to stop the flooding and send His mercy, Father Bergeron tried to help people in any way he could. "My favorite Psalm is 'the Lord is my Shepherd,' " he stated, "and Bergeron means 'little shepherd' in French-Canadian."

He continued to kayak around the area for several days. "Horrible things brought a lot of people together, which is for us to right our priorities, and hopefully this is akin to changing events by giving attention to the needs of others," he added.

H wanted to bring hope to parishioners and maybe witness to others who needed faith. A man of great faith and joy, he finds laughter in the darkest situations. "Even the attitude of kayaking in the midst of the storm is like the punchline of a joke. It is something surprising that hopefully brings a smile to the faces of people, hopefully calms their heart," he responded.

He added, "I know a hispanic man whose house was flooded. He was with his children and grandchildren, asking for help while sitting on a kitchen table as the water was rising. He sent me pictures of all of them sitting on the kitchen table- what a selfie!" he explained. It was a time of finding anything to smile about to add some levity to the dire situation.

"I have a shirt that I designed a few years ago 'KEEP CALM, PRAY AND PLAY." This symbolized what happened in Texas." He also used those words as his mantra and for inspiration.

He found himself praying in his kayak in the midst of a storm trying to be calm and sharing this faithful attitude with others. Father Bergeron conveyed hope and his unwavering faith.

"Christianity was brought by crossing the ocean - and I tried to bring it from my canoe," he stated.

Father Bergeron's brother, Francois, was in charge of the relief effort for the Catholic Charismatic Center as they distributed food, clothes, baby diapers and drinking water. The church is still doing relief efforts," he said.

He looks back at his kayak ministry with wonder. "I was getting texts from parishioners who had seen him on TV, and who told me, 'I guess we're alive, and the Lord is alive, and the Lord is always with us as well.' "

7 WATER

RESERVES CAJUN NAVY

"WE ARE THE HELP"

The Louisiana Cajun Navy was founded by Clive Cain, who is based in Louisiana. The not for profit consists of volunteer boat rescuers who came together and descended on Houston to help with the hurricane rescue effort in the terrible flood waters. They have a 230,000 following on Facebook and are a different and distinctive group from the Cajun Navy.

Their website states their mission:

'We don't wait for the help, We are the help! We the people of Louisiana refuse to stand by and wait for help in the wake of disasters in our state and the country. We rise up to unite and help rescue our neighbors! Our mission is to help the people who can't get help, not only in the wake of disaster, but in everyday life. From the underprivileged, the homeless, and all veterans in this country, we won't stand by and watch another person suffer, struggle, and fight for their lives, while the world passes by.

We're here to do something about it and make a real change in the lives of many. The words homeless and veterans should never have to be used in a sentence together. Louisiana Cajun Navy and all of the many volunteers and supporters, are here to make a difference, make a change, and to bring people, families and communities back to life and out of devastation!'

Cain made national headlines when he reported that a looter shot at a group of his volunteers and tried to steal their boats.

Here is Cain's story.

***

"I started a 501c3 after Katrina, Team of Hope, and I have been doing hurricane relief for about 13 years," he said.

His inspiration came during one of his first rescue efforts during the 1,000 year flood in Baton Rouge. His daughter Katie, age 29, was living in a mobile home with her mom and was scared.

"I went to rescue my daughter and some other people and along with Operation Barbecue Relief, we served 1,000 meals in about 13 days," he recalled.

He officially launched the Louisiana Cajun Navy after that effort and wants to leave a legacy for his other daughter Aja, who is a medical assistant and a member of the Navy.

Cain is no stranger to grief as he lost a son, Christopher Robin, who died in his sleep after taking a prescription medication. He became inspired to work at a faith based rehab center named the Wybuilders. His compassion and desire to help others in need during disaster became his mission.

Cain, who is also a photographer and graphic designer, said that the Louisiana Cajun Navy does everything from search and rescue operations to handing out food and hauling donated supplies.

When Hurricane Harvey happened, he was in the New Orleans area where he loaded his truck. "We grabbed some boats and drove to Pasadena, Texas, where we met volunteers with boats, special agents from the police department and some regular guys who used their boats for hunting and fishing," said Cain. They had posted on Facebook a call for volunteers with boats.

"The Coast Guard was receiving an estimated 1,000 calls per hour," US Coast Guard Lt. Mike Hart reported to CNN. On August 29th alone, the Coast Guard had rescued over 3,000 people and was overwhelmed. The Houston Fire Department had over 500 calls according to CNN.

"We rescued hundreds of people of all ages and backgrounds. "Imagine being in a hurricane for five days. Things were flying around and it was kind of chaotic," he said. "Sometimes I felt like I was driving on a lake when in reality it was a road."

There were cars and debris that were submerged under the surface of the water and there was the constant danger of a propeller hitting a unseen object. "Some of our boats got damaged and we had to rescue other boats that were damaged too," he recalled.

Cain, who is a Type 2 diabetic, and suffered from sleep deprivation and dehydration, put others first. "I can do all things through Christ who strengthens me," he quoted. He looks to God for security and to keep a clear sound mind.

A self-described adrenaline junkie, he said he never thought of the real dangers he faced during the rescues. "Sure, there were days I was going to quit, but I felt that I would be robbing people of service." Facing insurmountable challenges at times, he refused to give up. He put aside his own creature comforts.

He added, "There is no greater love than to lay down your life for friends."

For his service, Cain received the Ronald Gardener Inspirational Award, who brought the Super Bowl to New Orleans.

The Louisiana Cajun Navy is credited with saving hundreds of lives. "We are here to make a difference and a change, and to bring families and communities back to life and out of devastation!" Cain clearly walks the talk.

8 GOING ABOVE AND BEYOND: JIM MCINGVALE

"TEXAS LEADS BY EXAMPLE"

Philanthropist and businessman Jim Mcingvale, best known as Mattress Mack, made national headlines for transforming his high-end Gallery Furniture stores into shelters following Hurricane Harvey's torrential rains. Known for his generosity, he opened two of his largest stores to hurricane-displaced victims and accommodated approximately 400 people per store.

He also held a fundraising event for the Salvation Army with President George H.W. Bush and the late Barbara Bush working as bell ringers. Gallery Furniture deployed its largest moving truck to rescue people caught in the floods, and Mcingvale was praised as a local hero.

This is his story.

***

Jim first tweeted in the midst of Hurricane Harvey.

For residents in need of shelter who live near Gallery Furniture Grand Parkway and can safely get here: Gallery Furniture Grand Parkway is now taking in more people in need of shelter as of 5:30PM CST Tuesday August 29th, 2017.

Animals must be kenneled, and the kennel kept at owner's side. If you are in need of shelter, we invite you to safely join us at 7227 West Grand Parkway South if you can travel here safely.

Thank you to every volunteer, and our service men and women for their brave and unwavering compassion during this difficult time.

According to Mcingvale, he woke up with about two feet of water in his home and was immediately alarmed. He later arrived at his office and quickly made the decision to use his company's moving trucks to rescue stranded residents in their homes. He sent out a message on social media and people began responding.

Additionally his wife, Linda, who manages Westside Tennis Club, dropped everything when the hurricane hit and spent the next five days rescuing people by boat.

On Sunday alone, 15 or so Gallery Furniture moving trucks rescued over 200 people. People of all ages, from age 3 to 90, came to the store.

"Some people walked out of their houses carrying a trash bag with all their belongings," he said. "Many displaced residents came into our stores crying and we offered to help them."

Mcingvale and his employees handed out aid including water, food and supplies to the storm affected refugees. They also offered moral support and tried to assist with temporary housing and even jobs. Some of those camped out in the makeshift shelter even began helping with administrative functions and other tasks like handing out food.

"We gave jobs to some of the people who sought shelter in our stores because they had a great work ethic and were empathetic," he recalled. "We were working the hell out of our people 7 days a week to help people, and no one ever complained."

He pointed out that he is extremely proud of his employees who stepped in. They were clearly inspired by the resilience and strength they witnessed at the stores. "Our employees ran to the fight, not away from it," he pronounced.

There were some dark times but Houstonians according to Mcingvale "put up one helluva fight."

"God's love and our faith sustained all of us," he recalled. "There was light at the end of the tunnel."

His faith was reaffirmed time and time again when he saw the outpouring of generous donations from the community like baby formula and diapers. There was such an overwhelming outpouring of support that people did not feel like they were on their own and isolated during such a trying time.

One of his favorites stories was watching a young girl fill her backpack with candy that was stocked in the store. "Her parents didn't have any money so we gave her candy so that she could have a party with her friends," he said.

Although Mattress Mack cited the first responders as his heroes, in May 2018, he was honored by Interfaith Ministries for Greater Houston at its annual Tapestry Gala and a Change.org petition was created to honor Mcingvale by giving him a key to the city. There were over 40,000 signatures in his support in just under three weeks.

"Texas is a land of heroes like Davy Crockett, William Travis and Sam Houston, who all led by example," he explained. "Texas is color blind and its residents help regardless of ethnic background, race, religion or political party."

TEXAS HERO MARCUS LUTTRELL AND WIFE MELANIE LUTTRELL

"GOD BLESS TEXAS"

Marcus Luttrell, a decorated former U.S. Navy Seal and the author of the" Lone Survivor" was awarded the Purple Heart and the Naval Cross for his brave actions in 2005 against the Taliban fighters during Operation Red Wings. He's a Texas hero and a Lone Star Thriver.

He and his wife Melanie, helped to rebuild World War II veteran Lt. Bill Fly's home after it was destroyed by Hurricane Harvey.

In her own words, this is Melanie's story.

***

"We live in the North of Houston in Magnolia, and our road got flooded, but we couldn't leave because the bridge got washed away," she recalled.

They were stuck there for a few days until a neighbor came by with a construction type vehicle and built a temporary bridge so they could leave.

"He brought in a ton of dirt, and it was a temporary fix, but it was pretty amazing and so sweet," she said.

Marcus later posted on his Facebook page that his home was surrounded by water but was basically dry. A soft-spoken hero who was the only survivor of Navy SEAL Team FIVE, offered the following words of advice on social media:

"Find a swim buddy and watch each other's backs until this is over. Have a plan and a backup plan. Take care of yourself, take care of your family, take care of your neighbors, and take care of your town. DO NOT ATTEMPT TO DRIVE IN HIGH WATER, CALL YOUR LOCAL AUTHORITIES, they are out to help. If you are safe and dry, STAY SAFE AND DRY. God bless Texas."

Not only did a neighbor respond to the Luttrell's post with help, the Luttrells later passed on that good turn to another neighbor.

"We had not met those neighbors but they saw on social media we were stuck inside. I posted it on Instagram"

"A few days later, we got a call from the kids at the school our kids go to, Rosehill Christian, and some of the parents who had been volunteering in different neighborhoods," Luttrell recalled. "They came across Lt. Fly who was 99 years-old when we met him."

Melanie described him as fragile and frail. His wife had just died 3 months ago, and he didn't want to lose his house or lose his freedom.

"He is so self-sufficient - even drives to the shops and pharmacy, but he lost his car, and the house, in part, in the floods," she said.

"I told him on the first week of September that I was going to try to rebuild his house," said Luttrell.

Melanie's dad is in real estate, and she has helped with different projects so she felt confident about offering to help.

"I called a couple of friends, called my uncle Les in Atlanta to ask him if it were possible to rebuild the house," she recalled. "There was 5 ft of water in Lt. Fly's house, and he did not have flood insurance. My uncle Lex said, 'if you do it right, it should work fine.' "

She immediately thought of one of Marcus's friends, Keith Bell, who owns a company called Cotton, who does disaster relief for commercial companies.

"I knew he was busy and asked his opinion, and Keith told me to meet him at the house." He agreed to take on the project, and Melanie was ecstatic.

"Everyone fell in love with Lt. Fly," she said. "My kids fell in love with him instantly- they now think every old person is like him."

They started with one fundraiser online. Melanie posted on social media a video of Lt. Fly and raised $80,000 in a few days. People were so generous too.

"Some people gave up to $10,000 dollars- I don't even know who they are. They didn't even write a note," she recalled. "Others donated services, including an air conditioning company." She feels the people in Houston have a really big heart.

"I was raised to have a servant's heart - always help others, you never think of yourself in a tragedy, you always think of others," she said.

One of the granddaughters of Lt. Fly videoed his daughter telling him they were going to rebuild his home. "He just started crying- so emotional," she recalled

"People of all ages related to Lt. Fly, and some started to see their own grandfather in him."

They started off with one fundraiser and did several more after the first one. Several businesses stepped forward to help, including the owner of Gallery Furniture, Jim Mcingvale.

"Mattress Mack is a friend of ours. I called his daughter Liz, who donated the windows to the house," she said. "One of my friends from college, Steeler Lumbar, donated all the lumber, and a cabinet guy donated the cabinets. A granite guy donated the granite counter tops and so on."

The work of all who came together helped Lt. Fly get back in his home before his 100th birthday. They even worked on the house on Labor Day weekend to get it livable.

"Mattress Mack completely furnished his home," Melanie said. "We went to Target and bought all the linen sheets, silverware with the donation money. Target even donated $2,000 dollars."

While Lt. Fly's house was being renovated, Fly, his daughter and son-in-law stayed at Melanie's dad's ranch in Normangee, Texas. He asked Melanie to be in charge of the rebuild project. She chose the finishes and more as he trusted her taste and judgement.

"As soon as we finished the house on Nov. 9th, we planned a homecoming and 100th b-day party for Lt. Fly."

In November, Lt. Fly came back to his house for a combined unveiling and birthday party. **Fox 'n Friends** recorded the joyful event.

"We got to show Lt. Fly the house- he loved everything we did," she exclaimed. "He started crying."

They also surprised him the night of the house unveiling with a car. A donor from Austin, The Legacy Foundation, donated money to Melanie to buy him a car. "I was able to buy him a used Cadillac, and his face just lit up. He had never in his life had a Cadillac," she recalled.

An ecstatic Lt. Fly said, "A new house and a new car on the same day- I think I am in Heaven."

Texas Roadhouse, a big restaurant chain, also came out to the unveiling and donated $50,000.

Melanie said, "With Texas Roadhouse's money, I was able to rebuild two other veterans' homes." They helped Mr. Ferrill, 90, a veteran who served in WWII and the Korean War.

His wife and son passed away, and he doted on his grandchildren," Melanie said, "His house had 3 ft water, and he refused to leave the home." Camped up in one room, he used cold barbecue pits to cook. "It's really crazy," she recalled.

"He had a bedroom where he camps out, she added. "He only wanted a new kitchen as he'd take care of the rest!"

The Luttrells helped another vet, Marin, 94, who was in the army and fought in Germany. Melanie said, "He still has his army uniform from the WWII- he brought it out to show me."

Melanie's strong faith sustained her. "I pray everyday. I'm definitely a believer," she stated. "Since I was a kid I have asked GOD to help me help others. That prayer has come true so many times."

An answer to a prayer also came in the form of her husband Marcus, whom Melanie formerly-Juneau met through her dad. "Marcus told me the first time we met that he was going to marry me," Melanie fondly recalled. She added, "I loved everything that he was -extremely confident and so amazing - it's hard to find a man like that."

The Luttrells have been married 7 years and have two children. Melanie also has a son from a previous marriage. Marcus, who refers to Melanie as his angel, has openly spoken about the rough time he had when he returned home alone without his fallen comrades in Iraq. Former First Lady of Texas Anita Perry has been credited with helping Marcus find his footing and equilibrium.

"I was almost killed, I don't know how many times," Marcus said. "Just because I retired from combat life doesn't mean I can't stand up and fight, and especially when we get hit like this."

Melanie feels her mission is to help widows and the children of the fallen who have lost their way. "I want to help those find a way back from their grief," she explained.

Meanwhile, she and Lt. Fly have remained good friends, and she talks with his daughter multiple times per week. "He came to my Christmas party, and I went to his home for Thanksgiving," she said.

"My kids don't think I have a job because I don't go to an office," she laughed, but "helping others like Lt. Fly is my job."

Lt. Fly and his family are eternally grateful. "They cannot realize how much it's appreciated," said Fly. "I just think of all these people who came in and helped like they did and donated money to do what they could."

The Luttrells had topped well over $80,000 in a fundraising drive at the time of this publication.

9 OPERATION BARBECUE RELIEF

"BARBECUE IS A COMFORT FOOD"

Operation Barbecue Relief was founded by Stan Hayes in May 2011 in response to a need for relief efforts when a massive El-5 tornado struck Joplin, Missouri. The stricken community consisted of about 50,000 residents and killed about 140 people and injured about 1,000. Hayes lived about two and one half hours away and his wife, Amy, told him to get his barbecue friends and find a way to help.

The tornado's path was six miles long, and the National Guard and emergency personnel needed food. Hayes and volunteers from several professional competition barbecue teams answered the call and were able to serve 120,000 meals in over 13 days. Food was delivered to shelters, hospitals, senior living communities and even the Humane Society.

Since then, Operation Barbecue has responded to 45 disasters across the United States in 24 states including Hurricanes Harvey and Irma and the California wildfires. Since 2011, Operation Barbecue Relief has served 1.75 million meals for survivors and first responders. There are 6,513 plus volunteers.

This is Stan's story.

***

"When Harvey hit, there's a small group that makes the decision to stay or go," said Stan. "For me personally it was 'when and where are we going, not if.' "

Haye's focus was getting the job done. Once they came up with a game plan for deployment, they emailed their partners to help with the donations and other assistance needed. Like so many organizations, Hayes posted his needs on social media.

The team's next focus was logistics that included finding a location to setup, and store equipment, meat and the gallons of sauce. Their staging area was behind One Allen Center in downtown Houston. A large parking lot became a barbecue haven and volunteers came from all over Texas and nearby regions.

"The core group of our organization are all pit masters or grill masters but we also have volunteers---sometimes as many as 150," he explained.

He also explained that there are always at least two people from Servsafe, a national food handling organization that focuses on health and safety issues.

"Barbecue is a comfort food- if you lost your house, or God forbid, a loved one, and you get a hot meal that reminds you of the barbecues you had in your backyard, it can make you forget about the bad stuff in your life," said Hayes.

The group served over 372,000 hot meals in 12 days thanks to two main sponsors: Butterball and Seaboard. "No one could believe that we were serving free meals," recalled Hayes. They also served hot sides including corn, peas, rice and beans that were all donated.

"We use ole hickory pits large capacity smokers donated to us," stated Hayes. "One smoker can hold 800 pounds of meat."

The pit masters take pride in their product and use the finest ingredients including rubs. They serve first responders and other hungry displaced residents tender, mouthwatering barbecue cooked with a lot of love. 50 portions of food were placed on aluminum pans so if a group came in and said they needed 1,000 portions, they would be given 20 pans. Some people came in for 5,000 meals at a time. This was a whatasized meal on steroids.

Hayes remembered meeting and serving exhausted firemen who would pull up to eat. "I sat with an Assistant Fire Chief in Houston who had lost his house and had not been able to go home and help his wife and family," he said. "I was able to give him his first hot meal in days."

Hayes does not feel that the first responders get enough credit for all they do. "I met amazing firemen who risked their lives by doing high water rescues." The days are backbreaking for them." Stan said. "Our chefs also work long, long days."

Clearly mentally and physically exhausted after long days of serving and straining over the heat, Stan was also ready to rest. But along came Irma and then Maria. There was no rest for the weary. During Irma, Hayes worked with FedEx, the Salvation Army and other nonprofits to airdrop meals into the Florida Keys. "We called it operation BBQ Air."

They went on to try and help in Puerto Rico but were faced with logistical hurdles such as lack of power, limited flights and exorbitant costs.

"We also worked with celebrity chef Guy Fieri to serve more than 50,000 meals to those impacted by the wildfires in northern California.

For Hayes, he doesn't mind the exhaustion. "It's hard to explain the exhaustion and the exhilaration coming at the same time," said Hayes. "Many of our volunteers have done multiple deployments and some travel hundreds of miles."

He stressed that the impact they make on a community is why they do what they do.

BRENNAN'S OF HOUSTON

"LIFE IS SHORT. EAT WELL"

F amous Houston landmark, Brennan's of Houston, located in the downtown area, has been serving up famous dishes for 45 years. Owner Alex Martin Brennan grew up in the nationally acclaimed Commander's Palace, owned and passionately run by his mother Ella Brennan, a New Orleans grand dame. After training at La Varenne, Alex made his way eventually to Houston and in charge of Brennan's. Under his watch, the esteemed Brennan's of Houston has achieved the Exxon Mobil four-star rating beginning in 2000.

Alex and his sister Ti Adelaide Martin and cousin Lally Brennan have many new restaurant ventures including the Cafe Adelaide and the Swizzle Stick Bar in New Orleans and the SoBou in the W Hotel in New Orleans named Best Restaurant by Esquire Magazine. They have received several James Beard awards.

During Harvey, Alex and Ti Martin helped to rally support by the restaurant community. Over a five day period, Brennan's served 15,000 meals to first responders and to the Cajun Navy and to Jim Mcingvale stores and Methodist Hospital. The restaurant also cooked for those displaced in shelters.

This is Alex's story.

***

"During Hurricane Harvey, Brennan's had already taken on some water in one of its main dining rooms and some of the staff were dealing with flooded homes and cars," he said. "Many of the restaurant staff were living in parts of town that were under water and close to bayous.

Alex, who was home in Tanglewood when the storm hit, suffered minor damage to his property especially in comparison to other areas. His father-in-law, George Sims, lived by Lakeside Country Club on the bayou. As it had not flooded for 40 years, he had decided to stay.

"On Sunday morning, we saw the forecast and drove toward his home," Brennan recalled. "The area was flooded. I am 6'2, and the water was up to my waist."

They managed to get into the house and his son was able to take him out of harm's way in a high water utility vehicle. Once his family was secure, he headed to the restaurant and was greeted by a handful of employees.

Soon, word began to spread that food was needed for evacuees, first responders, hospitals and shelters. "We began preparing my favorite foods and made large amounts of jambalaya, salads, bread pudding and other popular items from our menu," he stated.

Brennan was sending the food out hot, but the need was so great that they quickly ran out of containers. They put the word out that they were in desperate need for food containers and suppliers sent trucks loaded with containers, plastic plates and plastic ware.

An employee put up on a website "CHICKENS NEEDED," and the response was immediate. "Our suppliers also brought in food, including Martin Foods who brought in 1000 pounds of chicken," he said.

They had large 40 gallon cooking kettles in the kitchen so they were capable of cooking vast quantities of food. "Chefs around the city were working with us in concert - our chefs including sous chefs Martin Weaver and Jose Arevalo worked tirelessly and one personally took food to Search Homeless Services," he recalled.

A need became apparent at Methodist Hospital System where doctors and nurses were without food for days so Brennan's donated breakfast tacos, fried chicken, gumbo and jambalaya.

"We even had volunteers come in to help including an accountant that I put to work cutting up vegetables," he laughed.

He stressed that Houston is a doer kind of city and giving back is just what you do. "We might be a country divided but Houston is not."

Wendy Warren, VP of Louisiana Restaurant Association, concurred. "The Louisiana Restaurant Association set up a Hurricane Harvey Hospitality Employee Relief Fund, working with the Commander's family of restaurants and the Greater New Orleans Foundation that manages many different charitable funds," she said.

They were awarded grants to hospitality workers in partnership with the Texas Restaurant Association and regional chapters. Some of the members collected 15,000 gift cards from restaurants and donated them to people in need.

In Wendy's words, "After hurricane Katrina, the Houston community was there for New Orleans, and we will never forget it," she said.

"Ti, from the Commander's group, called the day after the hurricane and was so humble - told me they don't want to do anything for the publicity," she added.

Ti went on to start a new fund for Harvey relief. Wendy sent a text message on behalf of the association to connect members and they hooked up restaurant owners with other owners to network to find out where help was needed.

"Our people are usually there even before the Red Cross shows up," said Warren. "They bring red beans and rice, jambalaya and huge roasted pigs and stacks of ribs."

They staged food stations in key areas like the convention center or churches and fed first responders and others.

"It's an emotional thing. People search out ways to connect, and unless you've experienced this, it's just hard to imagine. But many people in Louisiana have been through this."

"We had national chains and national suppliers with foundations wanting to do things and we want to help and be there when you need us."

8TH WONDER BEER

"CRAFTING GOOD BEER AND FUN"

In 2013, inspired by the spirit of Houston, Ryan Sorkey, president of Wonder 8th brewery, began brewing beer in a dome-like warehouse in East Downtown. Sorkey had been a student at Tulane University and had evacuated when Hurricane Katrina struck so he knew only too well the devastation a hurricane can cause.

From Sunday, August 27th through Wednesday, August 30th, Alex Vasilakidis, Robert Piwonka, Alex Piwonka, and Jack Nugent led rescue missions in the M939 5-ton 6 by 6 military truck they owned. It was purchased for a little fun and never presumed it would come in handy for hurricane relief. In the truck, they went to flooded areas with six feet of water and pulled people from roofs and flooded homes and transported them to dry ground.

From Thursday, August 3rd to Monday, September 4th, Ryan and other brewery members and friends assisted in post storm relief efforts including unloading supplies for the Houston Police Officers Union that was supplying the area with support as well as shuttling supplies from the two main shelters, George R. Brown Convention Center and the BBVA Compass Stadium, to smaller relief centers.

They also donated a portion of proceeds from the taproom sales and donated to several local organizations including Houston Food Bank, Kids' Meals and the Houston Area Women's Center.

In Ryan's words, this is their story.

***

"A brewery is nothing without its community," he said. "In times like these, we have to give back and help out any way we can."

He explained that he and his wife had evacuated to Dallas along with their two year old son but came back to Houston after a few days. "I was worried about my colleagues and their safety and their needs,"

Along with his partner Alex Vasilakidis, they became runners for supplies to churches and other shelters as the Brewery was only a few blocks away from the Convention Center. It was a group effort and it was all hands on deck.

Ryan had previously purchased an old military truck, an M35 Deuce, to promote the 8th Wonder brewery. They never thought it would be used as a people ferry on flooded streets.

They started downtown but later went to the Fifth Ward and the severely impacted Meyerland area.

"I'm proud of my team," he declared. "There is a lot of damage in Houston but we will come back faster and stronger."

10 FIREFIGHTER PUTS OTHERS FIRST

"MY COMMUNITY COMES BEFORE ME"

Firefighter Kyle Parry is an EMT based in Lumberton, Texas where he works part time and also works full-time for the Beaumont Fire Station.

He lost everything during Harvey's devastating floods, but there was very little he could do. Like so many first responders, Kyle spent countless hours rescuing people and could not focus on the waters rising near his home. Among his belongings were everything he and his fiancé had purchased for their upcoming wedding including her wedding gown. Parry was focused on his mission: helping others in the area. He worked 14 plus hours a day and had no idea that his home was flooded until a friend sent him a photo.

His story demonstrates one of many shining examples of responders putting others first. It's the **Hurricane Factor**.

This is Kyle's story.

***

The Hurricane hit, and Kyle's first thought was service, not his upcoming wedding.

Parry settled in Lumberton in 2013 after he decided he needed a change of pace. Prior to that, he was living in Canada where he met his fiancé, Stephanie Hoekstra in high school. In Lumberton, he knew a friend from high school who was a firefighter and started to volunteer. After two years, he earned his certification.

"We sat a wedding date of September 10th in Galveston but have postponed the wedding," he said. Harvey interfered.

He was working so many hours that he was unaware of how he had been personally impacted. "I have lost everything in Hurricane Harvey but my sister-in-law and two sisters started a GoFundMe account, and I will rebuild and get back on my feet," he stated.

He was working nonstop and did not get home until August 31st to survey the damage. Parry filmed his home on Facebook Live, where he walked through waist deep water amidst floating tables and chairs in the brown water. In the video, he said, "This is where all the wedding supplies were," as he panned across the linens, table centerpieces and decorations he and his fiancé had bought. They were all floating in the water.

Stephanie had brought her wedding dress to Lumberton two weeks prior to the hurricane, and it had been in the closet. Parry had never seen it until the hurricane was looming. He had placed it on a shelf out of harm's way and had grabbed Maggie, his rescue dog, and her 6 puppies along with his lab Fiona and taken them to the fire station.

The only thing left was the dress. He was worried about it but had to put his personal feelings aside.

His job as a firefighter clearly came first.

In Stephanie words, "I spoke to Kyle during the week, and I was so worried, but he stayed in touch," she said. "He would call me from his personal truck when he was doing rescues."

She added, "I am so proud of him, that he puts others first."

The dress miraculously survived, and Stephanie was elated. Parry enjoys being of serviceto others and being on the front lines.

"I love it here- I have a dream job working for the best fire department in Texas," he said. "My brothers and sisters in the First Department all helped me- we are one big family, and no matter what happens we are fighters."

The expression "Iron sharpens iron" applies to Parry and his fire department family.

While this love story didn't end in marriage, both Stephanie and Parry learned what was important in a chatoic uncertain world - Love for one another.

11 GOD IN THE MIDST OF THE STORM

"GOD IS BIGGER THAN OUR STORMS"
LUKE 8:22-26

With God, all things that seemed impossible were possible during Harvey. 60 churches opened their doors to Hurricane victims and many other faith communities helped with relief efforts and fundraisers. This list is a endless. Volunteers from Our Savior's Lutheran Church, LDS charities from the Church of Jesus Christ of Latter Day Saints, Cross and Lutheran Church in Georgetown, Champion Forest and Baptist Church, La Grange Church of Christ and many other churches across the region collected and donated food and supplies to assist displaced residents.

The Jewish community was particularly hard-hit by Harvey according to the Jewish Post news. Seventy-one percent lived in neighborhoods with heavy flooding. The Jewish Federation of Greater Houston was impacted significantly by the flood waters and received a letter from Benjamin Netanyahu, Prime Minister of Israel, who wished the members safety and well being. The Evelyn Rubenstein Jewish Community Center (the city's only JCC) was flooded with ten feet of water. Chabad provided kosher food shipment through Amazon and the members of lsrAID also coordinated a relief and aid campaign.

Taryn Baranowski, marketing officer for the Jewish Federal of Greater Houston said in an interview to the Jewish Post that 12,000 seniors were affected and that it would take a long time for recovery. She stressed that they are a resilient community and "people are already banding together, they're working with each other to help recovery."

One of many countless examples of church and synagogue communities coming together was the incredible response effort at St. Martin's Episcopal Church in Houston. The largest Episcopal Church in North America, St. Martin's, is also the home church of President George H.W. Bush and the late Barbara Bush. She was a member of the Saintly Stitchers, a group that provides beautiful needlepointed pew kneelers. My sister-in-law Karen Garrett is a member of the group and remembers fondly how friendly Barbara Bush was. "She posed with me for a selfie and I cherish it," Karen says.

According to Church pastor, Dr. Russell Levenson, Jr., she rarely missed the Monday morning stitching meetings when she was in town. Dr. Levenson gave a powerful eulogy at her funeral and pointed out her amazing strength and faith. He joked that both President George W. Bush and his brother Governor Jeb Bush told him to keep it short. "I'm long-winded at times but I watched the clock," he said.

Dr. Russell Levenson, Jr. witnessed many acts of kindness and compassion among his parishioners. He has seen his share of hurricanes, including Ivan in September 2004 where his previous parish, the historic Christ Church in Pensacola, Florida suffered severe damage in the belfry and the nave.

These are Dr. Levenson's words.

***

"As I learned in Florida, you get through it by pulling together," he said. He felt it was their parish's responsibility to reach out to those affected. St. Martin's had very little damage but the surrounding areas were impacted. The Texas church community supported their efforts and many work crews came in from other areas including the Church of the Incarnation in Dallas. St. Martin's also hosted those who came on mission trips from other churches across the country.

Parishioners cooked meals, did laundry, took up donations and acted as prayer partners. "I get a lot of the credit but I don't deserve it," Levinson said. "Anytime someone came up to me with an idea, I said 'sounds good' and got out of the way."

He preached a sermon on a Sunday after the storm and asked for a show of hands by those affected. He observed that some people were reluctant to admit that they had storm damage. They didn't want to burden others. Some even felt guilty because their homes were intact.

"I preached and I gave out verbal permission slips stating that its okay to feel any way you want to feel," he stated. "I said that if you were feeling anger at God or guilt, that it was okay."

He did not want anyone to feel alone, isolated or targeted.

"While America at times is defined by its division," he stated, "in Houston, we are defined by our diversity and our united teamwork during crisis."

Dr. Levenson witnessed the outpouring of love and God's blessings for many weeks post-Harvey. He was also taken by surprise by an incredible offer from American actor and philanthropist Gary Sinise. "I received a text from him asking me if we were okay and he later followed up with an offer to headline a concert for Harvey relief," he said.

After the 911 tragedy, Sinise formed the Lt. Dan Band to support first responders and military personnel. The band has performed at USO shows around the world and hosted numerous concerts. He also performed at the 2018 National Memorial Concert.

With the support of the Gary Sinise Foundation, American Airlines, Bayou City Center, St. Martin's Church and St. John the Divine Church, a concert was held November 12th, 2017 at the Bayou City Event Center.

"Gary discussed with me the idea of giving away tickets as a way to help first responders and to give light and support to the community, he said. There was also a fundraising aspect with a text-to-donate number.

Kristin Massey, vice president of the Bayou City Center, lost her home in the hurricane but refused to charge for the venue. HEB provided food and all proceeds went to the St. Martin Church's Harvey Relief Fund.

St. Martin's Episcopal Church put forth their best when some were impacted the worst. 400 of the church's members signed up on Sunday mornings to volunteer, and many more helped to clean worksites, serve dinners, do laundry and research, and attend discussion panels. Thousands of items and the amount of monetary support was astounding. 13 mission teams were hosted from around the country.

People gave this of themselves. All of their time, effort, and resources went to repairing and helping their community. Even those who had lost everything helped. 100 parishioner families helped who were impacted by the flooding themselves.

"Post Harvey, we saw America at its best," Levenson exclaimed.

YEHUDA KAPLOUN, PRESIDENT OF WATERGEN USA

"EVERYTHING THAT HAPPENS IS GOD'S WORK"

Watergen has developed unique and advanced technologies to extract water directly from the air, our most abundant water source, using innovate GENius™ technology. GENius™ is the world's first and most energy-efficient Water-From-Air module of its kind (efficiency-size-cost ratio), generating water a 2 cents per liter or 250Wh/L.

Among the advantages of this technology are:

- Can be easily scaled up or down to any size required. Each ½ a meter produces about 2 liters/hour

- Produces 4-5 times more water per kW

- Small size. Can replace other heat exchangers currently installed

- Low-cost structural materials

Yehuda Kaploun served as the President of Kap Consulting Group with offices in North Miami Beach and New York City.

He also served as the Executive Vice President of the Moses and Aaron Foundation, the organization created by Nobel Laureate Elie Wiesel that serves children with special needs, since its inception twelve years ago.

Mr. Kaploun has assisted in an advisory capacity in New York to Mayor Giuliani, Governor Pataki and New York City Comptroller Thompson along with other community leaders. He has been a Director of Pop N Go Inc. since April 2008.

Watergen worked with the American Red Cross and FEMA in the United States to assist people in Texas and Florida by providing clean and safe drinking water in the aftermath of Hurricanes Harvey and Irma.

Watergen along with a team of Watergen technicians traveled to the U.S. to deploy, operate, and maintain two large scale and two mid-size GEN-350 units. The units were first set up in Port Arthur, Texas where a water reservoir was contaminated by Hurricane Harvey, and the people in the area lacked clean and safe drinking water.

In response to Hurricane Irma and with the direction of FEMA and the American Red Cross, Watergen then moved operations from Texas to Florida. During that week, the units dispensed clean drinking water from the air in Miami-Dade County and also distributed drinking water supplies to Broward County and the Florida Keys.

If you took the Empire State Building, more than a hundred stories tall, you could fill that entire volume 33,000 times with the water that fell on Houston and the surrounding areas. That shows you how much rain there was.

In Yehuda's words.

***

"We sent Watergen units, the machines that make water from air, from the U.S. and air freighted from Israel two large scale units in."

Post storms, the systems generated 5,000 to 8,000 gallons of water a day, depending on the humidity. "We were giving out water to thousands of people." When you have a crisis like Harvey, people show up day or night to get water. "The beauty of our system, when equipped with power and generators, is that every day we could give out water," he added.

Texas Houses of Worship became the center for people and made certain that their neighbors were covered. "There definitely was a lot of Texas pride. This was the first time I was part of a humanitarian mission. We were able to rent mobile homes and stock them with food to provide for Americans who had lost everything because Israel is such a great friend of America, and vice versa, and of course having a great pro-Israel president," he recalled.

Yehuda witnessed an incredible spirit of cooperation during their time in Texas. "The amount of carnage that was there was remarkable. The first responders did an incredible job given how bad it was. I think that Brock Long, FEMA and Jeffrey Dorka did an incredible job in very trying times. They were available 24 hours a day." He remembers one instance at 3 or 4 in the morning when they didn't have the right cable. "They were there for us," he said.

Israeli Billionaire Michael Mirilashvili and Ed Russo were actively involved. "As people, we know how to relate, thinking in times of crisis and doing what needs to be done," he reflected.

"I grew up in a house of doers. My father's father moved from Israel in 1967 and passed away on the eve of Rosh Hashanah, the Jewish New year." He remembers, "All of a sudden, there were knocks on the door. People were looking for him. Unbeknown to us, he had delivered food packages for years and years to those people to make their lives easier. None of the family knew about these deeds of kindness before," he recalled.

Yehuda learned to give back by, not just one grandfather's example, but from both patriarchs on either side of his family. "My mother's father was an emissary of the previous Lubavitch Rabbi. He was a Rabbi for 50 years and ran a Jewish Day School in New Haven, Connecticut. When he heard there was a destitute family with a young student 40 minutes away, my grandfather drove every day to take him to school. He was the headmaster, chief fundraiser, and more of the school, and yet, he drove every day out of his way to pick up one student."

His father also demonstrated compassion toward others. "My father was no different. In every crisis, he showed up to help. We grew up serving people as a family. We learned that we are not just placed on the earth for ourselves."

And he continues this service in his daily life. "I have a program in Florida where I give out to 250 families all the fruit they need for the Passover. There is no greater honor than to make sure people have food for Passover."

"He who saves one life saves the world."

PASTOR RUDY RASMUS/BEYONCE

BREAD OF LIFE INC.
"FOR I WAS HUNGRY" -MATTHEW

R udy Rasmus is a pastor, author and humanitarian with a passion for outreach to the world's most challenged communities.

Today, he co-pastors the St. John's Church in Downtown Houston with his wife, Juanita.

A church that began with just 9 existing members in 1992, St. John's has grown to ministering to thousands of people every week of every social and economic background who share the same pew. He attributes the success of the church to a compassionate group of people, who have embraced the vision of tearing down the walls of classism, sexism and racism and build bridges of unconditional love, universal recovery and unprecedented hope.

He has generous support from a collaboration of government agencies and a significant donation from Tina, Beyoncé, and Solange Knowles. The St. John's Downtown campus includes the Knowles-Temenos Apartments, a 43-unit single-room-occupancy development designed to provide permanent living accommodations for formerly homeless women and men.

Temenos' CDC portfolio also includes an 80-unit apartment community to meet the growing need for permanent supportive housing for the previously homeless in Houston, Texas, and a 15-unit apartment project for chronic inebriates and the most vulnerable homeless individuals in the Houston community.

18 years ago, Kelly Rowland teamed up with Beyoncé and Tina Knowles to build the Knowles-Rowland Center for Youth where community empowerment activities for the young and old take place every week.

The facility is currently serving as the base of operations for Hurricane Harvey relief efforts.

Pastors Rudy and Juanita founded the Bread of Life, Inc., a non-profit corporation, in December of 1992 and began serving 500 meals per day to the homeless in the sanctuary at St. John's.

Years later the Bread of Life has changed the landscape of Downtown Houston, providing an array of services to homeless men and women.

The project also distributes over 9 tons of fresh produce weekly to hungry families. St. John's is one of few faith communities in the U.S. providing HIV/AIDS testing to churchgoers on Sundays through the innovative "Get Tested Project."

For many years Pastor Rudy has coordinated domestic and global anti-hunger initiatives in conjunction with Beyoncé's concert tours. He travels extensively developing and supporting programs around the world for people experiencing poverty. Today, with a focus on social impact investing, the Bread of Life owns and operates Eco-Life Employment LLC, a digital employment and staffing agency for men and women with troubled past lives, and the Amazing KMAZ 102.5fm radio station.

August 29, 2017 - Beyoncé gave a statement to her hometown paper, The Houston Chronicle, pledging to aid relief efforts for Hurricane Harvey.

"My heart goes out to my hometown, Houston, and I remain in constant prayer for those affected and for the rescuers who have been so brave and determined to do so much to help," Beyoncé wrote. "I am working closely with my team at BeyGOOD as well as my pastor, Rudy Rasmus at St. John's in downtown Houston, to implement a plan to help as many as we can."

This is Pastor Rasmus' story.

***

"It was my wife Juanita's example and spirituality and love that led me to the path I am on today." Rudy and Juanita have been married for 32 years and are the proud parents of two outstanding daughters, Morgan and Ryan, a phenomenal son-in-law, Hamilton, and an amazing grandson.

"One of my daughters is a psychiatrist, and the other is a psychologist. I think it's one of the benefits of growing up in a soup kitchen - which is what my wife and I did when they were kids to give them a great perspective."

He met Beyoncé through his mother. "Her mother Tina was my wife's hairdresser in the early 80s. We became friends as a result. We knew Beyoncé when she was born. She grew up around us. When we launched the church in 1982, she sang in our choir as a teenager. When she was 5 or 6 years old, she displayed a unique talent. We knew it was something special. Many years later we have seen that talent manifest, and the world has seen who she is."

Beyoncé contacted Rudy when she saw the story of elderly people in Dickinson floating in water. "She saw that story, called and said she had to do something to help people in Houston," he said.

"Her team came to Houston, including her publicist Yvette Noel Schure and her Director of Philanthropy Avy McGregor, as an advance team to see how she could use her brand and relationships to make a difference. She notified her high profile friends like Tyler Perry and Ludacris, who donated a lot of money early on and helped us get the word further out."

"Where ever there has been a need in Houston or anywhere in the world, Beyoncé has always responded. She is one of the most generous, loving people I know. Her mother raised her with a faith perspective, and she has not let go of that."

"For I was hungry and you have given me something to eat. I was thirsty and you gave me something to drink. I was a stranger and you invited me in. I needed clothes and you clothed me. I was sick and you looked after me. I was in prison and you came to visit me." - Matthew 25: 35-36

KC FOX

'DO UNTO OTHERS
AS YOU WOULD HAVE THEM DO UNTO YOU'

TV Executive, KC Fox, a graduate of Harvard Business School, has many different and vital roles as co-founder and strategist at American Black Cross. The American Black Cross was born out of the chaos of Hurricane Harvey. KC Fox is also Vice President at NAACP, Dallas and the president and social-political strategist at TLG Group. She is the CEO of The Vault International Firm. A firm specializing in media training, brand strategies etc. KC also founded the Lady General Foundation.

A former Air Force Sergeant wounded in Iraq, she lives in Dallas.

Hurricane Harvey left Houston and surrounding areas in shambles. Residents lost cars, homes, houses of worship and, worst of all, loved ones. The images reminded many of Hurricane Katrina's destruction in 2005 in that those affected were once again disproportionately black and brown. And many of those who were unable to evacuate or get out were tragically poor women and families of color.

But as the nation's fourth largest city begins to rebuild, a brigade of everyday citizens has been compelled to lend their help to the cause. KC and her co-founders, John Dixon III and activist Corey Hughes, deployed to Houston and Beaumont with a convoy of 25 vehicles. They enlisted 200 plus volunteers and three million dollars worth of goods and services.

This is KC's story.

***

"When we got on the ground just a few days after [Hurricane Harvey] hit, my immediate feeling was of survival - like I had landed in a combat zone."

Hundreds of Hurricane Harvey victims braved the heat to wait in line to receive goods.

Fox and her co-founders - attorney Lee Merritt, business mogul John H. Dixon III, and social activist Corey Hughes - witnessed it all. "We are empowered as a people. We do have the power and the influence to get these things done. We helped well over 6,000 people in 5 hours. We have the power to shape our own destiny. We do it with boots on the ground," said Fox, a former Air Force Sergeant who was wounded in Iraq.

She and her cohorts did something amazing within days after Harvey made landfall. Their initial convoy to Houston included 25 vehicles, consisting of an 18-wheeler loaded with requested items, three 26-foot U-hauls, two box trucks, a mobile medical RV, a mobile barber and beauty RV and several charter buses transporting goods and volunteers.

"You put aside selfishness and you uplift and build. Everyone doesn't have the opportunity to be as fortunate as we are. The black community needs stewardship, movement. I was a nurse at age 20 and started in health care and preventative medicine," Dixon said. "We need a Black American Red Cross. One that helps us when we need help directly and compassionately."

The Dallas-based task force enlisted over 200 volunteers, including people who travelled from across the country to assist.

Since their initial foray into Houston, the task force has garnered over $3 million dollars worth of goods and services, delivering 10-15 thousand packages every two days. The task force also deployed resource services consisting of clergy, attorney, barbers, nurses, psychologists, sociologists, babysitters, chefs, and financial and mortgage professionals.

"We have the ability to help ourselves. We can do it ourselves. We must take responsibility for our own community and be the change we want to see. We are on our own now. We are powerful. It's on us, and we got it," said Merritt. An attorney, he is well-known for taking civil rights cases, including that of the young black man falsely accused of being the Dallas sniper in 2015 and heart wrenching cases like that of 15-year-old Jordan Edwards, who was shot to death by police while sitting in a car with friends in 2017.

Pastor Renee Hornbuckle of Dallas is part of the ministry team that went to Houston, and she left hopeful. "The one thing that has made us successful in our effort is that we put aside our personal agendas and picked up a unified vision. I call us the 'unity convoy.' We are stronger together; a unified effort has created a unified force for doing good."

Although recovery efforts have now shifted to hurricane relief in Florida, the Caribbean and soon Puerto Rico, Houston must not be forgotten. It is critical to the rest of the nation because it is a diverse and international city with stellar universities, biomedical research, and energy producing industries. For example, over 30 percent of the nation's oil and gas comes through Houston.

KC also went to the Virgin Islands and Miami to help. "It became this huge machine."

For her, "this was more rewarding because I got a chance to see the people who were affected and got to see the fruits of my labor up close. To be able to see the little kids, dance with them." In the military, there is limited interfacing with people you help, not as relaxed. Some of the threats you face in Iraq, you don't see face-to-face in the military."

"I taught in the military mission planning for getting ready to be deployed so this exercise in Houston was a military operation."

"We brought to Houston clergy, attorneys, social workers and entrepreneurs to help people find work. We took bilingual individuals. Once we got there we set up deployment teams, even had inflatable boats to rescue people. I left no stone unturned."

"The State of Texas is very patriotic. It takes really good care of their veterans. I'm get chills talking about it, getting back to the moment calling people for help. A hundred plus people showed up with goods, water and supplies. A guy came to our compound and wrote me a check for $3,000 to get what we want. There are still good people who come together for the greater good," she added.

12 MUCKING AFTER THE HURRICANE

"I KNOW WHAT IT'S LIKE TO WORK HARD"
-BO DUNCAN

Austin resident Bo Duncan is the founder of STAV Creative, a firm that provides illustration and publication design, web design and branding and creates connections to help businesses grow audiences and build sales. Bo graduated cum laude from New York University and also founded the popular blog, ThreeDietsOneDinner, based on paleo recipes.

Her family members were affected by Harvey and she organized a local drive to provide art and other supplies to Houston area YMCA's and shelters. Along with her husband Cameron and their son Donnie, they also put in significant sweat equity by offering to muck out neighbors homes. Cameron also went into heavy hit areas like Meyerland and knocked on the doors of strangers and offered to help assist with the backbreaking task of removing personal possessions from flooded homes.

Bo's compassion and Texas Strong qualities were on display post Harvey and is one example of the true grit can-do Texas qualities.

In her words, this is Bo's story.

***

"Labor Day. It used to mean that school was starting, we had a 3-day weekend, or that you couldn't wear white until May. But now, to me, it means something bigger. It means work. Labor. Hard labor. This Labor Day weekend, I went back to Houston to help clean up after Hurricane Harvey," she said.

"I'm a business owner, and a mom of two boys. I know what it's like to work hard. And being from Houston, I know what it's like to clean up after a flood. But nothing could have prepared me for what Hurricane Harvey left behind."

"It is through tears and aching fingers that I begin to write this. I've been trying to understand why returning to Austin after just four days in Houston is so hard, but I think I see it."

"In Austin, life is going on after Harvey. And in the rest of the country, life goes on as others are waking up to what's left of their property in Florida. People have moved on-back to work, back to cooking dinner with their families, back to happy hour with friends, back to the gym, back to school," Bo said.

"In Houston, the Texas coast, Mexico, the Caribbean, and now Florida and Puerto Rico, life is not back to normal, and it won't be for some time," she explained.

After Harvey made landfall in Texas on Friday, August 25th, they had their first evacuees set up camp at the Left Right Media office: two friends from Cinnamon Shore in Port Aransas and a cat, Tina. Harvey hit Port Aransas and Rockport that night, taking with it many homes and businesses, some of them belonging to her friends there.

Harvey headed to Houston on Saturday night. Bo said, "My parents were talking about evacuating, but decided not to at the last minute. And by Sunday morning, most of my family's and friends' homes in Houston were underwater. My brother, Colin, got 9 feet. My parents' first home in Timbergrove, which they bought when they got married and rent out now, flooded 2-3 feet. My best friend's house in Bellaire got 4 feet, as did my cousins, and we watched the water rise around their feet (via Facebook) over the next few days." They were rescued by boat. Her Aunt Donna, who remodeled her home exactly a year ago, had flooding up to her brand new kitchen counters.

After the water rose, her brother went to stay with his friend, Tyler. "There was nothing they could do but wait until the water receded, so in a moment when the sun was shining, they decided to skateboard down I-10, something I'm sure very few people can say they've ever done," she laughed.

"I wanted to be there so badly, but there was no way in. Thinking back - Houston was like New Orleans after Katrina, and my mom, Lynn Hoster, was a school nurse in their pop-up "Katrina Schools," I remembered her telling me how scared the kids were for weeks after the trauma. Being displaced and through a flood, and now with parents who were either constantly on the phone with FEMA or trying to figure out how to put their lives back together, the kids needed help to express feelings through a creative channel. We thought art supplies would be a great thing we could contribute to these families."

They started collecting items with a simple social media campaign. "I couldn't believe how people responded. People I hadn't seen in 15 years (including my middle school gym teacher) showed up on my doorstep with donations. The drive brought in so many crayons, colored pencils, paper, school supplies, activity and coloring books, board games, crafts-you name it. The support and outpour of generosity from our Austin neighbors was incredible. And Houston needed it," she said.

"The following Friday, we Tetris'd my Tahoe with supplies, my baby, Harris, my best friend who lost her house in Bellaire and her dog, Bear, and we headed to Houston. Driving towards the George R. Brown Convention Center, which was the main Harvey shelter in Houston, was surreal. Downtown was quiet, except there were some people wandering outside of the shelter, approaching cars that were full of donations, asking for specific things-"Do you have any size 10 sneakers?" she added.

It took 15 teenagers to unload her car, and there were enough supplies to stock the shelter and 30 Houston area YMCAs that had lost everything.

On Saturday morning, Bo and her mom went to work on her family kitchen at her home in Timbergrove. "I didn't understand the devastation until we drove into the neighborhood. I couldn't breathe. It was a war zone. It smelled like ammonia and mold, and there were cars and people everywhere. There were piles, 7 feet high and 25 feet wide, of everything-sheetrock, flooring, broken furniture, wet mattresses, clothes, lamps, cribs, cabinets, appliances, toys, TVs, everything," she recalled.

Her mom's house was the same mess. "When you go through a flood, it's not over when the water goes down. In fact, that's the beginning. This is when the "mucking" starts. Mucking is the word we use for flood mitigation, which is the acceptance of the fact that all your belongings are destroyed, and they need to be hauled to the curb so that you can start ripping out every wall, built-in furniture and the flooring in your house."

When they got to the house, there was a flyer from a neighbor asking them to join neighbors for hot dogs on their front lawn at noon. Inside, there was another flyer from the Baptist church, with a phone number to call if you needed a volunteer to help you muck. This was the evidence of compassion that was already beginning to emerge from the rubble.

"She had already mucked, so what was left were nails, studs, and miraculously, her 80-year-old kitchen cabinets. What's left behind must be disinfected with harsh bleach containing a germicidal agent to stop the mold from growing and rotting your home. After the scrubbing and disinfecting, my mom and I just sat in lawn chairs and talked for an hour. She needed that most," she said.

Floods are not just physically destructive. They are emotionally devastating. "Everyone has a different way of dealing with things, and this causes so much stress in families. Some people are paralyzed by the destruction, and some people are energized by it. Some people run, some people cry, some people just pour out love. But everyone is emotional."

Later, her brother picked Bo up to take her to his townhouse. "He got 9 feet, the whole first floor. This is the fourth time his house has flooded in four years, and by far the worst. Driving into his townhouse complex was so sad. Everyone was outside hauling their soggy furniture and sheetrock to the street. Inside my brother's place, it was torn down to the studs. You could see through his living room, bathroom, laundry room and kitchen if you were standing in one place. The TV he was so proud of when he bought it was dripping water from where it hung on the wall," Bo said.

According to Bo, the overriding question was 'what's next?' "Do I rebuild?" she asked. "Where do I stay now? Is this building going to be condemned? Everyone in the complex has a long road ahead with insurance claims, FEMA, temporary and maybe new permanent housing, replacing lost contents. And since everyone is in the same boat, the waiting time for any relief could be weeks, months-and if it becomes a FEMA buyout-years."

She added, "seeing my my brother Colin's townhouse just broke my heart. After mucking, there isn't much my brother could do. And seeing him there, I felt helpless too. I can't take the burden away from him, but if I could, I would."

But, among all of the loss and sadness, she witnessed so much community, compassion and giving among neighbors, with no expectations of having the favor returned. "It's a beautiful sight. We saw that next at the cookout we were invited to by a flyer earlier that day. There were people of all ages there, sitting at card tables in chairs they brought, scarfing down hotdogs and chips in ravenous hunger. They were strangers becoming friends."

Bo's best friend, Christine, also lives in Austin, but they grew up together in Houston. She still owns a house in Bellaire, on a street called Dorothy. "Dorothy got a lot of water. I went over there after we left Timbergrove on Saturday afternoon. She had recruited (via Facebook) eight guys to help her muck. My boyfriend from 6th grade, who I hadn't seen in 17 years, was there. It's so strange to meet the adult versions of old friends you only remember as children. But here they were, just showing up to help."

"I told her I was bringing supplies, but for Christine, that meant a mini-ice chest with wine and charcuterie. We set it up on her brand new kitchen island, which was really her refrigerator that had fallen on its side. A Solo cup of wine in one hand, a crowbar in the other, we tore out sheetrock. If you've never done that with your best friend, you're really missing out on an incredible bonding experience."

After she left Bellaire, she called her friend Mariana. Her sister was in town and wondered if they were working at a friend's house. "She said to meet her at Catherine's in Meyerland where they had been for a few hours. We worked there for a little while together, hauling soaked Christmas decorations and knocking out walls. When I asked her how she knew Catherine, she said, 'I don't.' "

Bo was struck by the unselfish acts of kindness from strangers who pitched in to help other strangers. "On the way home, this all started sinking in. The magnitude of destruction here. The long road ahead that everyone had, but most importantly, the generosity of people. My mom called me when I was driving, asking if I would join her for church in five minutes. I tried to explain to her how sweaty and filthy I was. I had moldy drywall in my hair and floodwater in my socks."

Bo felt needed at church, so muck and all, she went. "We had a lot of prayer work to do, too," she added.

She later went back to her parents' house to meet her husband Cameron. "We had about an hour before we were going to meet them for dinner, so our next muck session needed to be nearby. We found a home in Braeswood with a couple who hadn't even opened their doors since they were rescued days before. We introduced ourselves to Harini and Sandeep, the owners, who had a lot of questions about where to start," she recalled.

"I pulled Harini into the front yard and gave her "the talk." The talk was the same one I remember my mom giving me when I was a kid and we had to do flood mitigation at her rental home. I had to have this talk with Catherine, the woman in Meyerland just the day before."

Bo said the "talk" is a bit of tough love and not easy to convey to someone impacted by the storm. "Everything has to be removed from the house, and most of it will be trash. We are going to move quickly, and we're going to throw it into a garbage pile in your yard. It may seem like we don't have respect for your possessions or the memories they hold but that's not it. Everything is collecting mold, and if we don't get it out now, it will make you very sick. After the items are out, we're going to start ripping out the walls. Then the floors. And we will bleach what is left. Are you okay with that, and are you ready?" she carefully explained.

She was ready. This first stage of flood mitigation is emotional. The discovery of ruined items is intimate. "Before we touched anything, Harini searched the house for a photo album that her daughters had made her a few years ago. That was the only thing she couldn't live without. We worked together gathering piles of photos that had already lost their ink. They were beyond repair. There were thousands," she added.

"There were prayer books, cookbooks, yearbooks, financial records, medical files. It feels wrong to throw this stuff away. It also taught me a lot about who this family was. I learned that he is a doctor, their daughter went to my high school. I learned about the religion they practiced, the kind of food they cooked, the books they read, the clothes they wore. And by the end of the day, we learned the way they cried and fought with each other."

Bo told her that we would start by hauling out the most soaked items and furniture first. "This meant beds, pillows, couches, armchairs, clothing, bedding, etc. Then we would take the large furniture out. Even if some of the heavy wood antiques looked fine, they weren't. They were rotting, and they would not survive. Both she and her husband wanted to save a lot, but after the first few minutes it became clear to them that they couldn't."

Bo said, "She hadn't had a change of clothes in a few days, and didn't want to get anything new, so there were a few items she wanted to clean. This is true-you can save some clothes if you basically boil and bleach them. But to get to things, we had to pry the furniture apart with a crowbar, since the water had warped the doors shut."

Many sturdy items like pianos and refrigerators do not survive floods. "They wanted to save the piano, but pianos cannot be saved. In floodwater, they become tanks, and often collapse on themselves as they rot. They wanted to save their antique dining chairs, and we tried, pulling the "save" items in the backyard. Many of the legs just disintegrated when we picked them up," she said.

"We worked like tornadoes after the hurricane, and cleared out as much as we could in the time we had. We returned the next morning with more supplies and my son, Donnie-9, who was assigned pillow and blanket duty. We all had gloves, but he was the only one with a dust mask. Every store in Houston had run out of them, so we just did without. The mold was so strong our throats were sore and our eyes burned for days after."

According to Bo, couches, beds and area rugs are the hardest things to remove from a flood because they are waterlogged. "We had to destroy much of the furniture to get it out of the house, because you could only lift a fraction of it at a time. I can only imagine how hard it must have been for Harini and Sandeep to watch total strangers violently take hammers to their furniture. I kept apologizing in my head."

"At one point in the morning, a man named Scott showed up and just got to work. He was a stranger. Later, my cousin, Tommy, and Aunt Becky walked in the front door. It didn't matter that no one knew each other. You don't need an excuse or connection to help someone."

"We cleared the house and said goodbye. Harini was crying when we left. Their emotions were running high, and at this point, we were running on empty.

Bo then drove back to Austin, crying the whole time. "And the days following, I cried through the night, too. When you experience trauma with someone, even if they are a stranger, it feels like you become their family for a moment. I cried for everyone who flooded-my family, my friends and the strangers I just met. I cried for their neighbors. Houston broke my heart, and this is just the beginning of a long journey for everyone there."

She said hard times reveal some pretty amazing things in people. "Like a rainbow after the storm, people are going to show up. Through community, and through the goodness of people, we can move forward and move on. And if you can be a rainbow like that, grab a pair of gloves, a mask, a hammer and a smile-and just show up."

13 CREATIVE GIVING
"SMALL GIFTS HAVE HUGE RIPPLE EFFECTS"

Houston Independent School District announced that 9 campuses would be closed to repair damaged schools. Sheldon ISD closed four schools and the C.E. King High School was one of the hardest hit. Other school districts sustained damage as well. According to an article in the Houston Chronicle, School administrators estimated the costs at $700 million.

There was a generous national response to aid students and their families and many organizations donated supplies. There were also efforts from other schools' children and teachers to raise money and to cheer up others. The following are three examples of creative giving.

This is Caragh's story.

***

Arlington resident Caragh Magnus, age 4, might be the youngest Harvey philanthropist. She raised $600 by selling her drawings and leather crafts on social media. Her goal was to raise money to buy diapers and her fundraiser shopping spree purchased thousands of diapers, baby wipes and several containers of baby formula.

Her father, Michael, teaches advertising at the University of Texas, and her mother, Rebecca, teaches theatre at the local high school. They told Caragh about Hurricane Harvey in a way that a four-year-old could understand. She also watched some images on television and surprised her parents by offering to help.

Michael said, "She has a good heart and her immediate reaction was 'how can I help' -of course we were really proud of her and thought it was so cute." Since she loved to draw and do leather crafts, Caragh got busy producing wares to sell. She started over Labor Day weekend and sold 30 pictures in 3 days. "In 2 days, she raised $600." She drew pictures everyday before going to Kindergarten.

Her drawings sold for $5, and the leather coasters sold from anywhere between $10-$20. Some even donated more with the largest donation around $60. People from all over the U.S. bought her drawings.

They also decided to sell her art to victims of Irma in Florida and Maria in Puerto Rico. Michael said that she was surprised by people's response and didn't realize she could be so impactful.

Since then, she continues to create and sell art for charity. Through all of young Caragh's unselfish enterprising efforts, she has developed a large following. The Sock Monkey Junction, a toy store in Mansfield, hosted an art sale. "Most children don't show that kind of maturity," said Teri Smith, one of the owners.

"What Caragh has taught me," he said, "Is that I cannot think to myself that I don't have the resources ... if you can see a child raise money in 2 days, I can achieve anything."

READING THROUGH THE RAIN

"SMALL GIFTS HAVE HUGE RIPPLE EFFECTS"

Sarah Fitzheny is a librarian at Saint Anne's Belfield School in Charlottesville, Virginia. She saw an item about the website, the Hurricane Harvey Book Club, and organized a fourth grade class to post videos on Facebook of themselves reading uplifting stories for other kids.

"Reading the right book at the right time can change your life," she explained. Sarah approached a fourth grade teacher, McKenzie lnigoa, and together they started a conversation in the library with her students.

The children cheered up other children but also taught the rewards of helping others.

In Sarah's words:

***

"Our goal was to teach about empathy," Sarah said. "The first thing we did was to think about the project and to address the problem with putting ourselves in others shoes and then discover together how to help," she said. She sought to help the students understand the concept of empathy by talking about what those impacted by the storm might be feeling and experiencing. They showed pictures of children in shelters.

"I asked the kids if they thought they were bored, scared or sad," she said. Ultimately, they all agreed that the best way to help the kids was to cheer them up and make them laugh. She told them to select books and stories that matched their message. "The selected books all had happy endings like fairy tales and Elephant and Piggie books. We set up a recording studio, and they videotaped themselves reading the books."

They were posted on a website called "The Hurricane Harvey Bookclub." The electronic book club encouraged others to record their favorite stories and upload them onto the site.

"There was a beautiful moment when we showed them the videos of them reading," she recalled. "I don't think you can be a librarian without wanting to help people."

McKenzie said," It's empowering to be so young and figure out that you can make a difference in somebody's life."

LEATHER BECOMES
A LIFE LINE

A aron Helzer, owner of Maker's Leather Supply in Killeen, Texas is an ex-veteran. He and his fiancé, Janie Adair, started a fundraiser with the hopes of raising $500, but their expectations were exceeded as donations rose above $6,000.

In Aaron's words:

***

On August 29th, they posted on the Maker's Leather Supply Facebook page that they were starting a raffle. The post said, "These people have lost everything," followed by details of the raffle. In two hours, they had already raised $1,200. "We didn't think we could raise anymore money."

"As donations of leather-making tools and similar items grew, so did the offerings of prizes with eight people from the leather making community donating items considered valuable to people in the industry," Aaron said.

There were 500 evacuees in Killeen. Aaron said, "I gave the money raised to the Salvation Army as they assured me the money would stay in Killeen."

He said he cannot imagine living in such a way that you don't know where your next meal is coming from. "I like to think I am a good person and I had to do something to help,' he stated. "When the need arises, we will always do for one another."

***

Jim Linnell is another talented leather artist and teacher who lives in Venus, Texas. He teaches leather crafting online and decided to host a second online class as a fundraiser. Called the Roses for Texas, attendees paid $20 and learned to craft roses in leather.

In his words.

Linnell, who is retired, worked for 40 years with Tandy Leather Works- a chain of about 130 stores. "The class I taught lasted about two hours and I taught the students the tricks and secrets of doing roses," he said.

"People sent me the finished product to show me what they had done and I sent them critiques." Linnell raised a little over $1700 with participants all over the world including Sweden and Taiwan. He feels honored to have this gift and to be able to teach others.

"If you don't use the gifts you have, shame on you," said Linnell. He cites his wife Denise of 42 years as his inspiration.

His favorite saying is "Blessed is the man who is faithful in his work because he will stand before Kings.

14 TEXAS STRONG TATTOOS

"SHOW ME THE WAY"

Yahweh Approved Tattoos and Piercings is a Christian-owned tattoo shop in Liberty, Texas. They are locally owned and family-run by Maura and Mike Weems. A small studio, there are two full-time artists on staff. They had a creative way to help victims of Hurricane Harvey and further the Texas values of resilience and togetherness.

The tattoo shop offered $40 "Texas Strong" tattoos with a percentage of the sales going to a local family impacted by Harvey. Over the course of just one week alone, they completed over 50 Texas themed tattoos.

This is Maura's story.

***

"In 2011, the Lord put the opportunity in front of me to have a tattoo shop. I was always an artist, a painter. A friend of my husband got into trouble and went to jail so we got the opportunity to help the family out by buying the tattoo shop."

"Yahweh is God's name in Hebrew. God appeared before my husband and gave him the name for the business" Yahweh was considered the most sacred name of God in the Old Testament.

"We have a wonderful guy called Michael Armstrong who has a good heart, works with us, asked how can we help people as we have not got boats to save people- and he came up with the idea of the tattoo 'TEXAS STRONG.' "

"Our customers pay us, and we put a percentage of the money to help needy hurricane families."

"The people of Liberty are the most beautiful people, our house burnt down in 2001- and the whole community left brand new clothes on the lawn for our kids - such generosity of spirit."

"We don't have love within us. It's Jesus love."

"God is in me all the time. You can tap into Him and ask Him what to do."

They belong to small community church Jubilee Covenant Fellowship. "They are my spiritual parents. God used them to change my life and my children's after our house burnt down."

"God has so much love to give us. It's the way we work at it. We can shine like diamonds. We are the salt of the earth," she added.

"God's word is the living water that drives me every day. I can see now Psalm 16:11 - *'You will show me the way of life, granting me the joy of your presence and the pleasure of living with you forever.'* "

The Strong tattoos themselves expressed many personal sentiments. The tattoo images were a creative outward indelible expression of the lasting impression of living through a major disaster. "We saw 'Texas Love, Texas Strong' everyday for years. That's Texas; the world only got to see it after Hurricane Harvey."

15 KELLER WILLIAMS CARES

"TRADITION OF GIVING"

G ary Keller is the founder and Chairman of the Board of Keller Williams- one of the largest real estate companies in the world. Since its founding in the late 80's, the company grew to be the biggest real estate company in the Austin area. In 2014, Keller Williams reached the milestone of over 100,000 agents worldwide.

An author, Keller's first book "Millionaire Real Estate Investor" was a bestseller. A supporter of his alma mater, Baylor University, he has donated funds for a research center in the business school known as the Keller Center. He has received many accolades through the years including recognition by Austin Business Journal as one of "Austin's 30 most influential."

Gary also established KW Cares, a 501(c3) public charity created to support Keller Williams associates and their families with hardship as a sudden emergency. Their website states that "Philanthropy is based on voluntary action for the common good. Ours is a tradition of giving and sharing in the spirit of the family helping family that is essential to a better quality of life."

Over $20 million was contributed through KW for Hurricane recovery. Immediately after the storm, KW Cares sent three 18-wheeler trucks from Austin to a Houston warehouse where volunteers were waiting. Due to the hazardous roadways, what should have been a quick trip took three days. An army of volunteers was waiting to unpack food, cleaning supplies, baby gear, generators and other essential items.

The firm had 4,400 plus associates in areas affected by Harvey. Realtors supported other realtors and other firms like Re/Max, Exit Realty and Coldwell Banker teamed up to support their community. The National Association of Realtors, with 1.2 members, worked with the Texas Association of Realtors to provide immediate assistance and relief.

Kathy Neu, Executive Director of KW Cares, has been with Keller Williams for 25 years. She got into real estate to work with people. She moved to her current role in 2009, and is one of the biggest advocates for associates and local and regional leaders. Under her capable leadership, the foundation has awarded millions of dollars in grants to associates and family members in need.

Her role during Hurricane Harvey was to approve wires and send money to people in need. KW Cares is set up to send up to $5,000 in an emergency situation to people who need food, transportation or shelter. They not only gave emergency grants to their agents and immediate families but helped others as well. KW reached out to those impacted in Louisiana and later to storm victims of Irma and Maria. Some of their agents even rescued people in boats.

In Kathy's words:

***

Neu was born and raised in Austin and has a long and distinguished pedigree as she is a descendant of the Murchison family. Her husband, Brandy, is Area Director for the South Texas Region and their eldest daughter is a Keller Williams agent. Keller Williams is truly a family affair.

Brandy set up a command center staffed with hundreds of Keller Williams volunteers, agents and their families. There was 20,000 feet available for storage of all the emergency supplies. Neu said there were 700 to 1,000 volunteers working over Labor Day weekend.

"Everyone pitched in and worked so hard. Rachel Tang - Programs Director took a lot of calls and I had to beg her to give me a stack of people to call back," stated Kathy. "My whole team worked around the clock - 7 days a week."

Their agents and families also helped rescue others in boats and later helped muck out houses. "After a Keller Williams agent got his own family to safety in Houston, he got out his kayak and went back out to help others," she recalled.

She was saddened by the folks who didn't have flood insurance -especially those in the "forced flood zones." Water was gradually released in certain neighborhoods to take pressure off the nearby dams and created a secondary source of forced flooding.

"FEMA did the best they could but some families had over $250,000 worth of damage and FEMA could only grant a small percentage of funding."

Kathy says that her faith motivates her during crisis. A favorite scripture is Romans 8:28 "And we know that in all things God works for the good of those who love Him, who have been led according to his purpose."

A compassionate woman, she was deeply concerned for those extended Keller family members and kept them in her prayers. She does believe that God only puts on you what you can handle.

"It's not about the cards you are dealt but how you play the hand."

The foundation also helped out during Superstorm Sandy, Joplin, Katrina and even the individuals affected by the recent California wildfires. It's clearly the KW culture to give back.

KW Cares continues to give money to people whose houses were destroyed in Texas. While Irma was not as dire, their regional leadership in North and South Florida stepped up to the plate Keller Williams clearly takes care of its own people, an amazing example of businesses treating employees like extended family.

PART TWO

HURRICANE IRMA TIMELINE

Wednesday, August 30, 2017
The National Hurricane Center began forecasting Tropical Storm Irma. It began as a low pressure system in the Eastern Atlantic with winds of 48 mph.

Thursday, August 31, 2017
Tropical Storm Irma intensified as a hurricane early in the morning. Wnds were up to 98 mph and it was about 650 miles west of the Cabo Verde Islands. The Leeward Islands were in its path.

September 1 through September 3, 2017
Irma crossed the tropical mid-Atlantic and its strength fluctuated to up to 145 mph.

Monday, September 4, 2017
Hurricane warnings were issued for the U.S. Virgin Islands and Puerto Rico by 11 p.m.

Tuesday, September 5, 2017
Irma becomes a Category 5 storm with wind gusts up to 175 mph. By 11:00 a.m., the Bahamas issued a hurricane watch for the Turks and Caicos area.

Wednesday, September 6, 2017

The eye passed over Barbuda and the entire Caribbean was under hurricane watches and warnings. By 8:00 a.m., the eye passed over St. Martin and Anguilla is pummeled. By 2 a.m., the dangerous core of Irma passed over the northernmost Virgin Islands. By 8 p.m., the eye of the Category 5 Storm with 185 mph winds passed north of Puerto Rico.

Thursday, September 7, 2017

Hurricane and storm warnings were issued for Florida and the Keys. Irma then passed the Dominican Republic and by 8 p.m., it pounded the Turks and Caicos Islands. Sustained winds were clocked at 175 mph.

Friday, September 8, 2017

Irma is downgraded to a Category 4 storm with extremely dangerous winds of 155 mph. Its southwestern eyeball moves over the North coast of Cuba and makes landfall by 11 p.m. It once again morphed into a Category 5 hurricane. After passing over Cuba, it weakened and sustained winds dropped to 125 mph.

Saturday, September 9, 2017

Hurricane force winds were projected for the Florida Keys.

Sunday, September 10, 2017

Irma makes landfall at Cudjoe Key as a Category 4 storm. Winds were 130 sustained mph. It ultimately weakened to a Category 3 Storm at about 3:30 p.m. By 6 p.m., it was downgraded to a Category 2 storm but gusts of 142 mph were reported at the Naples Municipal Airport.

A tide gauge measured water 2.2 above which represented a 7 foot increase from the previous hour or so. The storm had left at least 27 people dead in the Caribbean.

Florida Governor Rick Scott warned in an early morning tweet. "Life threatening storm surge is occurring now in the Keys and is expected to begin this morning in Southwest Florida."

FLORIDA
STRONG
IRMA

"Irma is a big storm and we must be prepared."

"Irma is an unbelievable Hurricane and we're making sure everybody's getting out."

Governor Rick Scott
-Florida

16 ALONG CAME IRMA

"YOU ARE STRONG, LORD, AND ALWAYS FAITHFUL. YOU CAN RULE THE STORMY SEA. YOU CAN CALM ITS ANGRY WAVES." PSALM 89:8-9

God's storms are sure to find us even if we don't look for them. Weather is nature's great disrupter and you cannot always escape it. Your only choice is to stand up to it. There is the peace of God within the turbulence and the trials make you stronger or break you. Sometimes we feel like that if we pray for strength and build anymore character that we can package and sell it. However, during Irma and its aftermath, there were once again numerous examples of faith and resilience tested to the core during adversity.

Social media again played a major role including the National Hurricane Center tweeting out watches and warnings. Governor Scott and first responders tweeted out updates and Facebook connected those in need with others willing to help.

Hurricane Irma was relentless in its mercy when it pounded and pummeled the lower Florida Keys on Sunday, September 10, 2017. Waterfront streets were underwater and tree limbs snapped off by the 130 mph plus winds, mingled with debris. Sailboats and other small craft were adrift from their moorings. Conditions were hazardous and the area and its 25,000 residents were under a curfew from dusk to dawn.

The popular tourist destination was in peril and turmoil. A large part of the Keys' economy depends on tourism and represents a $2.7 billion industry. 5000 of the residents are permanent military and many were homeless.

"This is a humanitarian crisis, "Monroe County Emergency Management Director, Martin Senterfitt, said in a statement. "Help is on the way." The USS vessel Kearsarge and its amphibious company headed to Irma after helping support other military assets in Texas following Harvey. Some 8000 troops of the Florida National guard were activated to the Keys and to other parts of Florida.

The USS Abraham Lincoln made for the Keys with other support vessels. The 101st Airborne Division, dubbed the world's largest helicopter army, also deployed. The Air Force deployed an air bridge which is continual flow of large jumbo cargo planes that can move tanks, troops and supplies in rapid time.

Meanwhile, Miami-Dade area and Ft. Lauderdale and the surrounding areas were spared somewhat by the full force of Irma but faced challenges of their own. It was a tough week for many who were without power and air conditioning. More than 2 million Floridians had lost power with 845,000 Florida Power and Light customers in Miami-Dade County, an FPL spokesman reported.

Floodwaters inundated the streets of Miami especially the downtown financial area along Brickell Avenue. Social media posts showed a storm battered South Beach where floodwaters rushed into residential areas and business districts.

The Red Cross relief effort worked with Federal partners to help those directly affected. More than 7000 trained Red Cross workers helped thousands of people impacted by the storm. There were more than 55,300 shelter stays, 62,500 health and mental health contacts, over 1.4 million meals and snacks served with partners, and more than 1.8 million relief items distributed. The Red Cross would remain in the area for several months.

The Miami Foundation teamed up with other volunteer organizations and shared posts on where to find shelters and assistance. Numerous non-profits and community groups came together to provide relief. Restaurants stepped up to the plate and offered discounts, ice and power to those without. Many had blue plate specials for first responders or simply offered a place to charge a cell phone. Some donated percentages of their sales to hurricane relief efforts.

Like in Houston, when Country legends Clay Walker and George Strait and Beyoncé lent their talents to hurricane concerts and Harvey relief, several celebrities helped out including Justin Timberlake, Leonardo DiCaprio, Beyoncé, Selena Gomez, Reese Witherspoon and others. They joined each other in a special concert called Hand in Hand: A Benefit for Hurricane Relief. Proceeds went toward relief efforts for both Harvey and Irma victims.

Pets faced extraordinary hardships during Hurricanes Harvey and Irma . Some displaced pets showed up in cities like Chicago and states such as Connecticut. As so many people were found not to want to evacuate during Katrina because they did not want to abandon their pets, the Pets Evacuation and Transportation Standards Act was founded. National organizations like the Humane Society and the American Society for the Prevention of Cruelty to Animals lead the charge.

Smaller organizations also came to the rescue including the Humane Rescue Alliance in Washington, D.C. The HRA takes animals already in shelters in storm affected areas when Harvey hit, as an example, and eased the burden for its owners. There is now a large pet saving network and these groups coordinated staggering number of rescues during Irma.

As witnessed during Harvey and its aftermath, the **Hurricane Factor** was in full force in Florida. There were hundreds of acts of neighborly love and compassion. Irma once again brought out the best in people, and those qualities that distinguish Americans as patriots and beacons of light.

Florida Governor Rick Scott was praised for his efforts. State Rep Shevrin Jones -D posted on Twitter @FLGovScott did a great job! He activated the state 911 plan and its resources. While recovery would be a long, slow and costly process, Scott assured shell shocked Floridians that he would help secure HUD money and other assistance for his state.

U.S. Representative Ron DeSantis-R said, "After going so long without having a hurricane, we on Florida's east coast faced two major storms in back-to-back years. What I remember most was the tireless work of so many people on the local level, both the emergency managers as well as folks who volunteered to help those in need. It almost seemed like it was second nature. I have no doubt that lives were saved as a result."

The Florida Strong delegation of Congressmen and Senators like Marco Rubio (R-Fl), hosted comprehensive recovery centers in St. Augustine, Jacksonville, Ft. Meyer and across the region. His staff was available to help residents sign up for assistance by FEMA.

Florida's Senator Nelson praised authorities' "seamless cooperation." President Trump signed a $15 billion hurricane relief bill that faced few obstacles passing.

17 MARC BELL
OPENS HIS HEART

"AMERICANS ALWAYS STEP IN TO HELP. IT'S A FLORIDA THING."

Marc Bell is an American financier and entrepreneur. He is managing partner of Marc Bell Capital, a Boca Raton, Florida based firm founded in 2003. He is also a producer of plays, musicals and movies. He is a former owner of Penthouse Magazine and sits on the Children's Village Board.

SOS Children's Villages offers long-term care for children in need in 135 countries including the United States with several facilities in Florida.

The Bells opened their home to one of the shelter's group of children who had no place to go following the storm.

This is Marc's story.

***

On Monday, Sept 11th, Marc got a 911 wake up call. "I got a call at noon from the Executive Director of SOS Children's Village (It's a foster home serving homeless kids for Broward and Palm Beach County) Jillian Smath, saying they were being released from their shelter and had no place to go with the 70+ kids they care for. Their homes had no electricity or water. They hadn't showered and had been wearing the same clothes for 5 days. They were hungry as they had not eaten yet. They needed help," Bell said.

He told Jillian to bring the kids over to his home in Boca Raton and together they would figure out a plan. "By 12:30pm they started arriving. As nightfall came we realized we could find no place for these kids to go, shelters were full and no beds were available," he stated.

"So my wife, Jenn, and I decided to allow them to stay with us for the duration and hence a very large sleepover began - 70+ kids and their house parents!"

He then posted a message on Facebook about what was going on and that he needed help. "Having 80+ houseguests last minute was a lot for me and Jenn to handle alone," he explained.

Marc explained that the kids, ages 2 to 17, had sleeping bags and slept two nights sprawled out in whatever room they picked. Groups of friends were able to stay together, which helped keep everyone comfortable in the new surroundings.

"We tried to entertain them all," he stated. "They were very sweet kids "

A generous man with a vibrant spirit, Marc said, "In life, there are those who talk about what they are going to do, and those who just do." He added, "When people need help, American's always step in and help. It's just a Florida thing."

And step up they did. "Over 100 of our neighbors came over to volunteer to help and made a huge difference between what could have been a disaster, and an amazing time for the kids," Bell recalled.

The Bells served 800 meals in 72 hours and did 36 loads of dirty laundry. They also arranged for 80 plus much needed baths and showers. Additionally, they celebrated 4 birthdays, had three doctor's visits and one tooth fairy.

For the birthdays, "We had singers, Bobby the Balloon Guy, Ziggy the Clown, School of Rock performers and also arts and crafts and manicures for the girls," Marc said. They also organized miscellaneous activities including football and basketball games. A masseuse donated some time as well. "The kids were in heaven."

He credits family, friends and neighbors for making it all happen. "Without the help of our amazing community, some of whom worked 16-hour days, we would never have pulled this off," he recalled.

Along with the Bells children, one 19-year-old and two 17-year-old twins, they served an abundance of meals including Chinese food, pizza, ice cream and cookies as well as some healthy foods like fruit.

"They got back into their homes late Wednesday night," he reminisced. "We turned a tragedy into a love-filled experience for these kids," he stated.

He enthusiastically said he would do it again in a heartbeat. And they are all asking to come back. "Of course we will have a more organized reunion very soon."

The Bells generosity truly made a lasting impression on these children's lives.

"I was very lucky to have had the opportunity and was blessed to do so. They will be doctors, lawyers, scientists - you name it!" But he added, "They will only get there with our help."

"We set up a GoFundMe page at https://www.gofundme.com/sosirma to help raise money to repair their homes and provided needed things for them. Since the storm between GoFundMe and checks I have collected we have raised $130,000. "

"The state only provides 50% of what is needed to house, clothe and feed these children. It is a huge tragedy is our own backyard. When we ask state legislature for more funding the answer is always the same and I will paraphrase: They don't vote, they don't give to campaigns, so we don't care," Bell explained.

"This tragedy of the kids being abandoned has helped raise awareness of our own plight, but this is a nationwide problem and not going away," he added.

Bell is concerned that "with an ever increasing population, the volume of homeless kids whose parents are deceased, incarcerated or unable to care for their children due to drugs, alcohol or mental issues, will continue to grow." SOS reaches more than one million families and children through its family care and support programs.

"These kids are our future."

18 OPERATION LINEMEN LAUNDRY LADIES

"THE LINEMEN IS A BROTHERHOOD."

Kelsey Murray, the mother of two kids, organized the project Linemen Laundry Ladies (LLL). Her fiancé Richard Whidden, is a lineman for Pike Energy Company.

Irma's severe winds knocked out several power grids and the Department of Energy dispatched 65,000 plus utility personnel.

She was looking for a way to help out linemen like Richard. On September 16th, she posted on her personal Facebook page that she needed volunteers to do laundry.

More than two dozen women responded and stood in line at Sebring International Raceway to collect the laundry of linemen. Thousands of linemen had traveled far and wide to assist with the tremendous challenge of restoring power.

The ladies collected the dirty clothes and took it to their homes to wash. The volunteer laundry squad did 94 loads of clothes the first night.

This is Kelsey's story in her own words.

***

"I understand what it is like to have a loved one far from home with no way to launder clothing," Murray said.

"The linemen is a brotherhood," she explained. "The staging sites aren't always the best because it is an emergency situation. There are no laundry facilities," she expanded, "and they have no time to wash their work clothes."

She added, "Many of the men have not had a chance to do laundry because they are working 16-hour days. Once we got power back on, we offered to do some laundry. It is our way to say thank you to them. We all take care of each other in the line life."

Women of all ages and from all walks of life have joined the LLL to make life a little more bearable for the linemen and tree trimmers that are working in the heat for up to 16 hours a day. According to Kelsey, many women began to take one or two loads home and bring them back the next day. Other women found it more efficient to take several loads to the laundromat in Lake Placid in order to process several loads at once

"The men bring their dirty clothes and they are put in a white garbage bag with their names, company, the date they are needed and a phone number to text them when the clothes are returned clean," Kelsey said.

She added " Eventually, the laundry tapers off if the staging area receives laundry facilities but until then, the women have done at least 150 loads of dirty laundry." The laundry was usually cleaned and returned the next day, however, in some cases, the laundry was done the same day. The LLL operates as efficiently as a one day dry cleaner but for free.

"The men are working long hours," "When they get back to the staging area at night, they shouldn't have to worry about doing laundry; they need to refuel their bodies with food and sleep"

Murray was inspired to help as her fiancé works grueling hours. "My fiancé is a foreman in Pike Electrical, he can't come home every day. The community always wants to feed people - so I decided to do linemen washing - I have heard stories of lines men who could not wash clothes for 2 weeks," she continued.

The first night they accepted laundry was Saturday, September 9th. She was at Sebring International Race Track in Highlands County, which was the second most devastated area in the State. "I rode the storm out in Highlands County, I stayed in Sebring, there was a lot of damage, power lines fell, down, wire cabling in the road, fallen trees. It took me an hour to get home. I stayed at a friends house when the hurricane was at its fiercest," she said

A Florida Native, she rode out Hurricane Andrew in 1992. "I now have 3 children 12, 10. 4 and it was scary for the kids, they think they are invincible - we prayed a lot that night. My 4 year old Adelyn sang a song EYE OF THE STORM, I videotaped it - Its a Christian radio song. It went threw my head many times," she recalled.

Fortunately, the kids were fine. "There were 10 people in the home, 6 were children 12 and under. We all slept in the same room: me and the children, and my friend's child, who is 12, slept in the bathroom in his room," she remembered.

The power went out at 6.45pm on Sept 9th and her fiancé Richard was part of the emergency crew in Sarasota County. "We were separated - but thats common," she said.

"We were able to communicate thru the entire storm, I started having trouble loading data from 11pm to 2am the Saturday night 9th on my phone," she added. "That concerned me."

Murray came back to her house the next morning Sept 10th. "I took my friend with me, as I didn't want to be alone, especially if the whole house was gone. There was a branch in my roof, the tree was 50ft away. - so we were very lucky. The tree was ripped around. The barn was destroyed, the power meter was ripped of - the pole fell down - all our power is a little messed up," she recalled.

Their power came back 11pm Sunday night so she was one of the lucky ones. "I was home for a few days, to get things cleaned up, and Richard came home for one day after the storm, and left at 4.30am the next morning to go to work. "It made it hard, me and the kids bathed in the above ground swimming pool. We took our soap and shampoo, my kids thought it was the greatest thing. They didn't like it being hot at night, but I had a generator, we didn't lose food."

Kelsey went to the race track at Sebring International Wednesday the 13th of September. The first thing she did was deliver pizzas to the Line Crew. "There was only one restaurant in the town that was open. I got the pizzas donated and delivered the food. That's how

I found out about the linemen guys who were stationed at Sebring international Race Track."

On Sept 14th, she went to the race track again and spoke to the Lineman from Duke Energy and asked them if they had laundry.

"On Saturday, Sept 16th I posted on my personal Facebook page that I needed volunteers from the community, to do laundry. It ended up making more sense to wash the clothes on site, I knew people who worked at the race track - they allowed us to be on their property to get the clothes"

"Linemen's clothes have a flame retardant on them so they require special handling - no fabric softener, etc." she said.

She had written down which lady had each laundry load. "The first night I was delivering back the laundry, I could not find 3 bags. It felt as if I lost my children." It transpired that other ladies had delivered the 3 loads she was missing earlier without checking them of her list," she said with relief.

Linemen, sweaty and exhausted, would pull their bucket trucks up, take off clothes from work that day, put in in trash bag with name, company and phone number. "

They washed 120 linemen clothes the first 24 hours. "We washed underwear, pants, shirts, whatever they would wear at night, running shirts, reflective vests, sweat rags, jackets," she stated.

"The second night we took all the loads to a laundromat - we were there till 1:30am." They got the detergent donated - everyone helped.

In a Facebook post that was shared, Jennifer Taylor Koukos posted an image of the volunteers. The picture went viral.

Murray, a nurse at a long-term care facility, works with the elderly - people who have had surgery. "It's a step down before they go home from the hospital"

"I saw the need for the linemen, and financially I was able to do this. I even declined working nursing shifts," she remembered.

"We are southern. You are not going to find people who don't want to help people here, and we are people willing to help everywhere your turn."

The last night they only took in 5 loads of laundry. "I felt I was spread pretty thin. It's very humbling. I'm not usually overly-friendly to people I don't know," she said. But she overcame her natural reserve to help.

Towards the end of washing the clothes, she was sleep deprived. "I asked people to pray for my sanity," she laughed

The part that was the most rewarding according to Kelsey was when the linemen came to get their clothes and offered to pay. "We would not take money from them - just asked them for a hug instead."

Kelsey showed her kids the news stories that had been shared. "I showed my daughter I was on Ellen Degeneres Nation. She was so thrilled"

A woman of profound faith, "We prayed to God all the time, 'please don't let us lose anything, or destroy their clothes.' You have to have faith or you'd drive yourself mad," she recalled.

Her reward was the gratitude of giving to others. "The guys are beyond grateful." And that's enough.

19 CARING FOR ISLAND DOLPHINS

"YOU CAN'T TAKE THE CONCH OUT OF ME," -DEENA HOAGLAND

Island Dolphin Care (IDC), was created in 1997 to help children with special needs and their families. The programs have expanded now to include adults, veterans and their family members. It serves those with developmental and/or physical disabilities, emotional challenges and critical or chronic illnesses.

Deena Hoagland, its founder, said "Island Dolphin Care believes that individuals with special challenges are able to participate in the full range of activities that life's experiences can offer and that everyone deserves the opportunity to play, giggle and have fun."

Hoagland was inspired to start the not-for-profit after witnessing the remarkable recovery of her son, Joe, who had suffered a stroke and had a weakened left side of his body. He began swimming with the dolphins at age 3 after not responding well to traditional physical, occupational and speech therapies. "Joe made tremendous progress physically and psychologically in a natural non-threatening and fun setting, "she said.

The dolphins work with veterans and others. The Dolphin Center took a tremendous direct hit during the Hurricane, and Phillip Admire, director of Zoology, and his wife, Michelle Crosetto, a veterinarian, remained in Key Largo. Like other pet owners or custodians of God's precious creatures, they were not abandoning their 8 sea charges.

The bridge in Monroe County had closed, and if they left, the dolphins would be alone and at risk. Thanks to their selfless acts the dolphins survived.

This is Deena's story.

***

"We took a massive hit with the hurricane and I had to be aware of my emotions and assume something good is going to happen," Hoagland recalled.

All eight of the dolphins stayed at the Center when the hurricane hit, and Hoagland begged Phillip and Michelle to leave. But they put the dolphins' wellbeing first.

Their buildings survived and the dolphins were okay but the water clarity was murky and thick with seaweed dirt. The freezers broke down, and they lost 20% of the fish they needed to feed the dolphins.

"There was all kinds of garbage at the bottom - we lost our docks, the cheekee rooms (an outdoor space), some educational exhibits our sensory gardens, security system, tidal pool, animal care hut, computers," she said. "It's ok. We will rebuild and be better."

She coped with faith. Hoagland's Center provides small miracles for those in therapy. "I am coping doing everything I can do to help everyone around me and I talk to God all day long, 24/7 I don't ask God anything as I wouldn't dare do that - I just say I look at this, I'm not sure I understand the reason. I'm sure I will one day," she said.

Hoagland admires the selfless sacrifices of Admire. She prayed, "God please give me the strength to cope with this and them too."

Research on dolphin therapy and autism have shown the impact of the unique interaction. People who are confronted with challenges, may get bitter or depressed, but not Deena. "I ask what do I need to do and how do I do this. Before you know it, everyone around you is there to help," she said.

Clearly she is also inspired by those her non-for-profit helps.

She's known hard times with her son. He has grown into a young healthy adult and also works at the facility. "You can't take the conch out of me," she laughed. "People don't always realize that they have a choice on how they are going to react to hard times and tragedy."

She said that dolphins could have a magic power to heal and that perhaps their healing power spared them all through the storm.

"Dolphins don't really have magic," she stated. "It's the power of love that heals."

20 MERCY CHEFS
"GOD HAS TAKEN CARE OF ME"

Ryan Watsche, of Elgin, Illinois, went with Mercy Chefs to help out during Hurricanes Harvey, Irma and even the California wildfires.

Mercy Chefs is a faith-based non-profit that is a disaster relief organization. According to their website, "We exist to serve professionally prepared meals for victims, volunteers and first responders.

Gary Leblanc is the founder and president. He stated, "We provide professionally prepared restaurant quality meals for victims and first responders in natural emergencies and natural disasters."

Mercy Chefs works with existing organizations within the community to maximize joint efforts. Their focus is not solely placed on immediate impact. Through partnerships, Mercy Chefs can and does leave a more lasting and permanent impact.

This is Ryan's story.

***

"All of what we do is donation based-no FEMA, or government money, only private donations or purveyors or chefs who come cooks with us," he said. Most of the Chefs donate food. They even had two gentlemen from BON APPETIT come in to help.

Ryan's business, Table Side Catering specialize in Mexican Italian Fusion with Custom menus for every client including vegan, Korean, barbecue, etc. "Comfort food is my thing," he said.

Despite a debilitating chronic illness, he gives a lot back to others. 'In 2015 I had a spinal stimulator installed in my back - it gives you control to give you impulses instead of meds. It worked well for 2 weeks but then got infected, and I got spinal meningitis," he said. Still, he recovered and keep going.

He also gives freely of himself. "I feed the homeless the first, third, and fifth week every Wednesday through First Congregational Church in Elgin. We average 65 people at a time."

"God has taken good care of me." He is in chronic pain but puts others first. "I look to my catering job to make money, and also it's my ministry. I employ people who need jobs: single mothers, homeless after rehabilitation, non violent criminals, people with bad breaks in life. And I love to work with veterans."

"I am looking to give people a chance in life," he added.

Three days before, Harvey, he had a dream. "I dreamed, 'you fed 10, you fed 100's now it's time to feed 1,000's' - it was God talking to me."

Then Hurricane Harvey happened. "I talked to my mom and said I think I'm going to have to go and do something with this hurricane," he recalled.

He went online and sent information to Samaritan's Purse, Feeding America, and Mercy Chefs. "I filled out applications for all 3, actually got a call back from Samaritan's Purse pretty quick but it didn't line up with my gifting. I am not a construction guy."

He gave it to God. "If I'm supposed to go, I'm going to go." Four days went by. Then he got a message asking how fast he could get to Houston."

Ryan flew into Houston, Sept 2nd and then took an Uber to Friendswood and hit the ground running.

"We set up at Calvary Chapel. The first couple of days I baked brownies, cakes and desserts - 100 containers of brownies, 80 containers of cakes."

He packed the food and the church delivered the food.

Mercy Chefs feeds body and soul with restaurant quality meals. "Without our volunteers, we would be nothing," he added.

"All the time I prayed to God, I asked for strength to be able to instill hope in others - every day to get another day because of my pain level with my back."

God answered his prayers. Ryan was able to work for 11 days straight. "In a disaster situation, if we have God, we can make anything happen as 'All things work together for the glory of God.' "

He witnessed people working together and strangers helping strangers. "Texans were helping each other, and out looking for people, rescuing people."

Many chefs turned up at Mercy Chefs, and they cooked 10,000 meals a day. "We had 3 or 4 entrees each course and had a lot of chicken. A purveyor gave us an 18 wheeler trailer of chicken - buffalo chicken, creole chicken, roast chicken - you name it, we did it."

"We had a donation from Hillshire Farms, a truck load of bread. I made bread pudding with biscuits, vanilla pudding, cherry jam - we even did cinnamon bread. Someone donated bagels so I made it with bagels one day."

FEMA representatives were in the church parking lot and people came by who had not eaten anything real in 3 days. "They loved the comfort food we make- our trademark at Mercy Chefs," he recalled.

They provided high carbs meals as they were trying to stay warm and rebuild their homes. "They need energy to work," he added.

Ryan needed energy too as Irma came along and they drove to help. During Irma, they stayed in East Florida - 15 miles outside North Fort Myers - and partnered with a church, Living Waters. "We always partner with a church, as when we leave there is a lot more work to be done," he said.

Mercy Chefs typically only stay 8 to 11 days until people get power back up. "We don't want to take business away from local business." And "when we are there, we try to eat out - the chefs are giving back."

During Irma, they didn't have power for 5 days. "We have generators and water so we are self sustaining. We fed about 8-10,000 a day," he said.

"We made spaghetti, meatballs, pasta primavera, chicken and desserts. Sometimes we get interesting things donated like Port Wine, a lot of hamburger type meat," he added.

A nearby resident with a swamp buggy took food from Mercy Chefs to deliver to people stranded.

"In Florida v Houston it was interesting on the socio economic side," he explained. "Florida was different. We were in the backyard of multi-million dollar homes in Florida. When you don't have power, it's the same as if you were poor."

"We cook based on an idea of what we are going to serve. The churches we partner with handle volunteers, dumpster deliveries, all the admin." The tag-teaming worked beautifully.

"There is a real camaraderie and sharing of the churches in Florida that they were helping one another - a relationship that was not there before." That's the **H-Factor.**

Ryan later helped during the California wildfires Oct 11th, 2017.

"I was serving meals to volunteers, police, fire and other public safety workers, members of the National Guard and U.S. Army and volunteers," he said.

They were stationed at the Christian Fellowship Church in Santa Rosa - half a block away from the worst devastated area where 1,000 plus houses were destroyed.

In the first 3 days, they fed police, fire, and national guard volunteers.

"We smelt smoke every day. There was a haze of smoke. For the first 10 days, it was ashy - we were constantly washing things off. We should have been wearing masks, but you can't wear masks cooking."

"Nothing could prepare me for what I saw there"

They were a half block from a 40 block area that was completely gone — 1,000 houses that were completely ash. "It was a hard day with people returning to see their homes completely destroyed."

"I posted a picture of a lunch for about 400 the group made one Sunday — oven roasted chicken, green chili cheese mashed potatoes, green beans with roasted tomatoes, smoked pistachios, sautéed onions and mushrooms and dessert pastry."

He performed a variety of duties in Santa Rosa, including cooking, cleaning, chopping food, managing volunteers, purchasing or procuring food and working directly with the managing chef to put together menus and organize the kitchen.

"I'm so grateful for all the amazing volunteers," of the people Mercy Chefs is able to find to assist with making and serving the meals.

"The people in Santa Rosa have been amazing, and many of them are crushed by all that they have lost, from homes to friends and family members." He felt honored to give back.

"I get blessed overjoyed by my work, when I see people's eyes after they have lost everything."

Ryan was away from home for 15 more days. He was tired but elated to help out others and grateful.

And he came away with some very valuable life lessons. "I learnt it can all be gone in an instant. Other than my family and my dog, it can all be replaced. God will give me better."

21 CLEARWATER POLICE

"GOING ABOVE AND BEYOND"

The Clearwater Police Department, under the leadership of Chief Daniel Slaughter, has 230 police officers and 100 civilian police and serve the population of 110,000 in Clearwater, Florida.

Clearwater is a beautiful beach destination with international visitors. There is typically some crime such as commercial and vehicle burglaries

When Irma hit, the Department faced many monumental challenges including restricting access to the Clearwater beach. As first responders, police officers and firefighters teamed up for debris removal to clear roads.

A photo of Officer Seth Stiers saying goodbye to his 7-year-old daughter in driving rain was posted by CPD, and it went viral far and wide.

CPD officer, Rob Shaw, a four-and-a-half-year veteran, like so many of his fellow officers, was able to help a 94-year old elderly woman. Rob's story was one of countless stories of bravery and valor.

In Rob's words:

***

"Rachel Copeland of Texas, post Harvey, was worried about the welfare of her 94-year-old grandmother Betty Helmuth who lives in Clearwater as Hurricane Irma set her sights on Florida," he recalled.

Rachel and her family had seen - - and lived through - - the devastating effects of Hurricane Harvey, and they weren't sure if their loved one was ok, so they reached out to the CPD.

Her grandma lives in an adult facility, which lost electricity.

Rob and other officers, including officer James Frederick, showed up at her door with food, flash lights and water. Notably, the Police Dept. paid for the food.

"Betty fell in love with them as quickly as they fell in love with her. It was like they were taking care of their own grandma."

"She was excited and tickled to see the boys in blue, but she joked that she was concerned her neighbors might think they were there to arrest her. She gave them all plenty of thanks, plenty of hugs, and called them her heroes," he said. Copeland said she was thrilled. "They are so good looking."

"We are glad we could be there in her time of need, to make sure she was safe and taken care of," he added.

"We here at the police department like to think we endeavor to be community champions - and that spirit and mindset was present the day late last week when we visited her."

According to Rob, Betty Helmuth is a sweet wonderful woman full of spunk and pizzazz.

"We went to visit her again after the storm, We have been there 3 to 4 times to check on her, and we get lots of hugs and are always offered tea. We say, 'just wanted to check on you.' "

"We love and adore her like our grandmother," he added. "She is the unofficial grandma of the Clearwater Police Dept."

Rob said Betty was especially taken with Officer James Frederick. "Officer Frederick has a 1,000 watt smile that lights up the room," he says.

Officer James Frederick said, "I paid for case of water, bagels, groceries and flashlights from the police department," as "Betty is so sweet. She has a friend for life. We are gonna check in with her every week."

"She is fun-loving, and one day, I will introduce her to my son, Cameron." Cameron had seen his dad on TV and talked about helping Betty and others.

"She was shocked when she saw us. 'Wow' was her first words. 'I have done nothing wrong' was her next."

He reassured her that theirs was a mission of goodwill, and they would arrest Irma if they could.

CPD Frederick has been an officer for 9 years in Clearwater. "I've been doing Community Liaison work for about a year - puts me working hand in hand in the community, closing the gap between community and law enforcement."

He said he talked to Cameron about helping others with needs and leading by example.

"I am faith-based. I do unto the world, I prayed for all the citizens to be ok in Hurricane Irma as I worked in shelters on the day of the storm."

Oak Grove Middle School was converted into a shelter. He worked 20 hours to make sure they were safe. "Most importantly, we were providing hope for people," he said, "and lots of people were comforted we were taking care of them - they were in a good place."

Families with animals were camped in the gym. Classrooms were equipped with ventilators. Brown said, "the kids and people they care for come first."

"We once had a firefighter whose house burnt down, while he was out keeping other people safe," he said. "He is still trying to put together the pieces of his life, trying to pick up the pieces of his life. No one could respond to the fire at his house in the beginning as it was too dangerous for him be out and about in the hurricane with severe winds."

He sees his purpose in life to 'DO THINGS FOR GOD'S GLORY.' "I don't do it for fame. I was raised by good parents and taught the way of the Lord."

Officer John Margnelli has unhesitatingly risked his life for others.

He has been at Clearwater Police Dept. for 10 years and is married with a 7-month-old child.

"I moved to Clearwater - after Fort Benning, Georgia. I was in the infantry. I was in Iraq 15 months in 2003. I was a sergeant in the army."

After the army, he studied Criminology.

"During Hurricane Irma I was in the main station in Clearwater, and we got activated into platoons," he recalled. "I was with 25 or 30 people. We handled 911 calls and helped people having issues with the hurricane. We went to shelters to check that people were ok," he said.

"In the car, it was me and a female officer (a new recruit). She handled it all well," he stated.

His wife evacuated with their child to Arizona for a few days. "It allowed me to do my job better- I was a police officer when she met me so she understood the job," he explained.

"The night the hurricane hit, all officers were pulled off the road. When the roads were deemed safe, they went back out. "I had brought my chainsaw with me. When I saw trees in the road, police were only on the road. I took it upon myself to cut the trees up into pieces"

At the end of the day, he was bone-tired after backbreaking labor. "The next day I felt my body had been hit by a truck," he said.

Power-lines were the main thing they had to look out for. "So we come down the street and wait for the Linemen to come - and move the wires or put the wires back together."

The outpouring of the community was generous. People brought food to the station, as thank you gifts. Working 12 hour shifts, the officers helped clean up yard debris and more. "We had a lot of power lights out. A lot of officers were used to direct traffic to help people- also doing ordinary police related matters."

He worked 5 days straight.

He also experienced the kindness of strangers. "When I ran out of gas for my chainsaw, there was only one gas station open. Some guy saw me with my gas can, called me over and filled my gas can for me."

Officer Margnelli had no time off. His personal life was on hold.

"The thing about hurricanes is it's our job as police officers, firefighters and first responders to go to work. We can't stay and help our own families. We sign up for it - our job is that of a first responder."

Like his colleagues, they just somehow kept on going. "When the hurricane was over, I took 3 days vacation to unwind. I slept 36 hours. I was beat. This is the hardest storm since I lived in this area the past 10 years," he said.

Everything got back to normal in Clearwater in a week.

SGT. SCOTT MYERS—CORAL SPRINGS POLICE DEPARTMENT

"LOVE FOR COUNTRY"

The police profession is often seen as a thankless career, but the officers in the Coral Springs force are appreciated by the community. CSPD was the only agency to receive the Award with Excellence in both Law Enforcement and Communications out of 100 agencies.

With a diverse workforce, there are 208 officers. There were dozens of touching stories of sacrifice and courage, including one of their officers stopping to pick up a flag in the middle of the storm.

On social media, the department posted, "Even in the middle of the storm, we are reminded of the love for our country and our community."

Coral Springs suffered severe weather including two days of pounding winds.

Sergeant Myers serves in the Crimes Against Persons Unit and the SWAT team and he and his team provided rescue and support service and risked their lives to help the community and deliver a baby.

This is Sgt. Myer's story.

***

"I was assigned to a 4-man team in priority vehicles. We were in a Bearcat -an armored vehicle used in SWAT CAT operations, so heavy it insulated us from the storm, allowed us to conduct operations when other vehicles weren't safe to drive," he said.

"I was responsible for 3 other people in the vehicle with me. Detective Brian Koenig, Firefighter Joe Schiavo, and Firefighter Yair Soto. Brian and I are SWAT operators. Joe and Yair are paramedics and firefighters," he added.

They spent the first couple of days after the storm getting back to normal operations, damage assessment, directing traffic where there were no traffic lights, etc.

"We were dealing more with obstacles and the wind issue as trees were crashing down. There was more wind than in Hurricane Harvey and we tried to minimize the risk by using the best equipment. We were all heavily trained officers."

They only went to calls that were worth the risk (ie if there is a suspicious incident call). "We had to prioritize the ones during the storm that were life threatening, giving birth calls, or when people's lives was in danger," he said.

"A tree crashed through a family's house - now, that family was at high risk. We rescued them and their dog and took them to a shelter." They were transporting this family when they got the call about a woman giving birth.

"The birth family called 911. Our emergency dispatcher who took the call, Lou Falco, knew the woman needed help. We were assigned to the call. Fire Chief John Whalen and firefighter Chris Hurst, who were nearer the woman giving birth got their a few minutes before we did. They assisted with the delivery in the bathroom."

"When we got there, the baby was pretty much all the way out… and the mother of the person in labor was actually pretty much delivering the baby - her own granddaughter - in the bathroom on the floor," assistant chief John Whalen, CFD, added.

Paramedics determined they needed to get the mom and baby to a hospital and transported them safely in the armored vehicle. "It was the first time a baby rode in the Bearcat."

The newborn was named April. "They were definitive in not calling her Irma," he laughed.

They faced a challenge loading her into the vehicle. "We opened the back up - we were able to slide the woman on a backboard in the vehicle and the baby was being cradled by a firefighter, Chris Hurst, who got in the the back of the Bearcat with the mom, and was able to sit with the mom and the baby." He said, "she kept asking how was the baby." It was a harrowing time for her.

"I am proud going on these missions. It's an honor to be making a difference, but there is fear and excitement involved too," he said.

Sgt. Myers, like many first responders, is a man of faith.

"I think when situations become dangerous and chaotic, we find the inner strength and drive to succeed. We become razor sharp, very focused, and want to do what's best for the community and our partners."

"Initially, my wife was concerned because she was in the middle of the Hurricane - she evacuated. We were thinking the storm was going into the East Coast, but it went to the West Coast. She got it worse than we did."

"When my wife found out we have delivered the baby she was excited," he added.

Sgt. Myers and his fellow officers put their lives and their hearts on the line on a daily basis. They are tested to the limit in times of crisis.

"Fear is healthy if you don't let it get the best of you," he stated.

22 MEDITERRANEAN GRILL SHELTERS OTHERS

"I FEEL GOOD FOR HELPING MY NEIGHBORS"

Gengiz Khan Restaurant and Mediterranean Grill is a Turkish establishment in Tampa. Its owner, Ergin Tek, came to America from Turkey in 2001. The son of a doctor, he came to study English and international politics but didn't have the appetite for his chosen studies. Ergin, in Turkish, means "someone who can take charge of their life." Take charge, he did.

In 2005, he started his restaurant near MacDill Air Force Base. It was named for his father, Gengiz. At the time, it was in a small storefront - about 1,700 sq ft and seated about 60. He brought in some talented chefs who specialized in Turkish and Continental food including lamb, hummus and other delicacies. Soon, it became so popular with nearby residents that he outgrew the space.

He relocated into a larger space on Bay to Bay Boulevard. It was a sprawling interior, and he worried that it might be too large. However, it's spacious quarters did double duty during Irma. After Irma swept through the area, the restaurant was converted into a shelter that housed and fed some 150 people. Gengiz Khan made international headlines.

A man who literally serves others - be it food or from his heart - Khan had helped the community during Hurricane Charlie in 2004. Charlie was the first of four individual hurricanes to strike Florida that year, along with Frances, Ivan and Jeanne.

Khan did community help and bought food for everyone in his complex. He gave out 500 plus cups of coffee and soda and fed homeless people. He also was prepared to do this during Katrina, but the storm missed Tampa.

He didn't stop there. Not only did he offer free assistance to others during Irma, he prepared thousands of turkey dinners for local churches and synagogues to feed the needy during Thanksgiving in 2017. Tek also staged Feed in Need, an interfaith nonprofit helping feed the hungry.

This is Tek's story.

***

"Because I have been through national disasters, I knew Irma was getting bad," he remembered. "If people died and I had not helped my neighbors, it would be awful. I would never have a happy day again in my life."

He had been preparing to help with Hurricane Harvey relief efforts and was planning a fundraiser when Irma's menacing storm loomed in the horizon. "I was really scared as it was very serious," he recalled. "I also didn't want to be selfish and make a few extra dollars from a fundraiser."

His restaurant is a stainless steel structure and a very sturdy construction. He decided to convert the space into a temporary shelter and posted his shelter plans on social media. The response was incredible.

Khan said, "Within two days, hundred of people came to me." He purchased generators, food, drinks, batteries, pet food and paid extra rent. He had enough food for about 10,000 meals in the restaurant. The setup cost was about $20,000, a large outlay of cash.

"Initially, we had potatoes and onions- that's the start of a good soup. I didn't want anyone to die of hunger if things got bad in Tampa."

He had about 152 people staying there along with 62 pets including cats, parrots and dogs. People came in from as far away as Key West. "There was a 39-year-old pregnant woman and a 95-year-old elderly woman who had been stuck at the nearby airport and could not get out."

He also drew up a plan to allow for a helicopter landing site in the parking lot.

"This town has been really good to me, and how could I not return the favor? We wanted to make sure anybody in trouble had a place to go. We were like an SOS who was ready and able to feed others."

"I even bought fluorescent paint to paint a cross in the parking lot so we could be spotted by rescue crews in case things went from bad to worse," he recalled.

They converted the shelter back to a restaurant after the storm but it took about 10 days to get things back to normal. After the cleanup, he still had leftover food.

"The food I had left was non-perishable so we gave it to the neighbors and the homeless."

A modest man, Khan does not feel he deserves any special credit for what he was able to do. "I will feel good forever because I helped my neighbors. It was a privilege from God."

A TALE OF TWO SYRIAN SISTERS

"SHARE WITH THE LORD'S PEOPLE WHO ARE IN NEED. PRACTICE HOSPITALITY" ROMANS 12:13

Sisters Abeer and Nora al-Sheikh Bakri, fled their homeland of Syria in 2010 and settled in Georgia four years later as refugees under the United Nations World Relief Program. Both of their husbands work—one is a truck driver and one is an electrician.

They had strong memories of what it was like to be refugees in Egypt and wanted to give back by cooking and donating their food to those affected by Irma.

Their desire to help others in crisis was, in part, motivated by their appreciation of those who helped them in the U.S. They didn't have a lot to give but gave of themselves.

Spoken to an interpreter, this is their story.

***

Nora said "I was so afraid when we heard about the hurricane, especially us Syrians. We're already traumatized as memories of leaving everything behind haunt us."

Their passion is cooking, and they knew people needed to eat. So they cooked tabouleh, mandi, chicken and rice dish, ground beef and vegetables and maamou - shortbread cookies with figs nuts and brought it to serve those in need.

"We wanted to be able to help these people so that these people can feel happiness. So they don't feel uprooted like how we felt."

The mosque wanted to pay them for cooking. "No way! We were humbled and honored to do this. We don't expect any kind of reward. We don't want anything in return."

They feel thrilled to be in America. "People have been so good to us since we came here," Abeer said.

PHOTO GUIDE

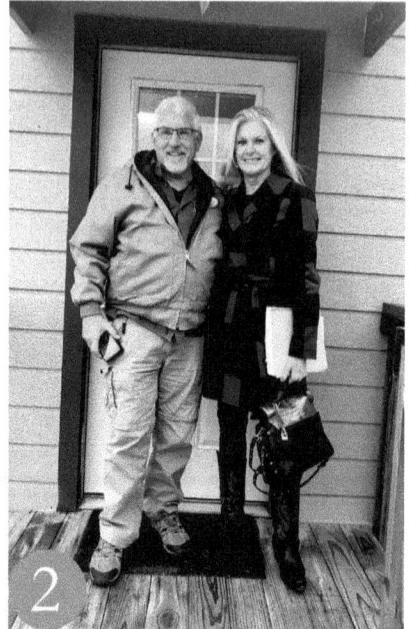

Foreword - Sutherland Springs

1. A memorial in Sutherland Springs as a tribute to the 26 victims.

2. Mica Mosbacher visits Pastor Buford.

3. Senator Ted Cruz offers encouragement to Pastor Buford of Sutherland Springs.

4. Church in Sutherland Springs.

Texas Strong   Governor Abbott visits Beaumont.
(Photo credits- Office of Governor Abbott)

Chapter 1 - Harvey Hits Texas

1. A Houston Home is consumed by Harvey's floodwaters, a flood of Biblical proportion.

2. Victims rescued during Hurricane Harvey.

3. 1000's of people were stranded in their homes during Hurricane Harvey.

4. Victims of Hurricane Harvey are rescued by helicopter.

5. Mica Mosbacher and Red Cross Shelter Supervisor .

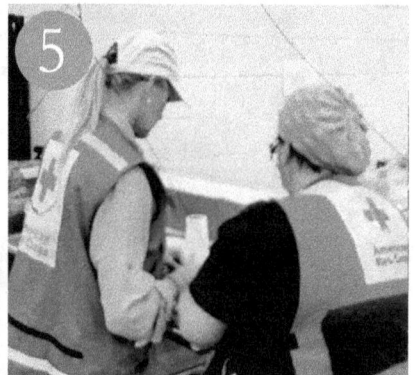

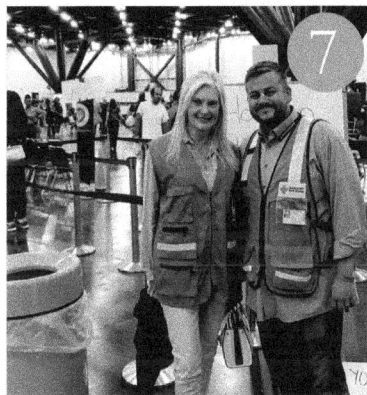

6 George R. Brown Shelter Red Cross volunteers.

7 Mica Mosbacher and the Red Cross Coordinator at the George R Brown Convention Center.

8 George R. Brown Convention Center was filled with donations for Harvey victims.

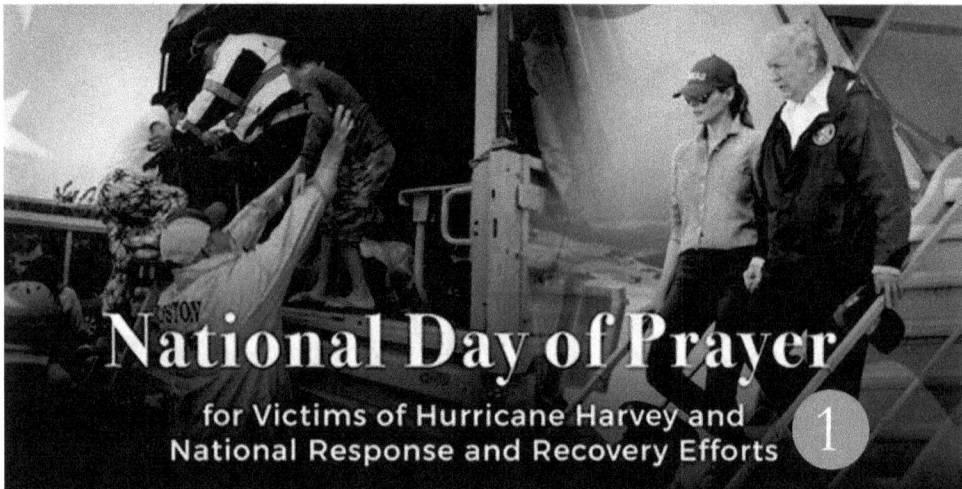

National Day of Prayer
for Victims of Hurricane Harvey and
National Response and Recovery Efforts

1

Chapter 2 - The Trump Factor

1. Trump's announcement of the national day of prayer (Including a visit to Texas by the President and First Lady).

2. Florida Governor Rick Scott Visits JFO in Puerto Rico (Photo Courtesy of FEMA.gov)

3. Vice Adm. Karl L. Schultz, commander of U.S. Coast Guard Atlantic Area Command, and Congresswoman Sheila Jackson Lee prepare to take part in a flyover to view areas impacted by Hurricane Harvey. Congresswoman Jackson Lee flew with the aircrew to assess the ship channels, ports and affected areas in Houston and surrounding areas. (Photo Credit WINGS:Women's International News Gathering Service)

President Donald J. Trump participates in a briefing on Hurricane Harvey's recovery efforts. (Official White House Photo by D. Myles Cullen)

Vice President Mike Pence helps move debris during a visit to an area hit by Hurricane Harvey, in Rockport, Texas. (AP Photo/Eric Gay)

Chapter 3 - Beauty in the Suffering

1 Aric Harding's playing a waterlogged piano for his son.

Chapter 4 - Harvey's First Responders

1 Houston Officer, Late Norbert Ramon, helped Hurricane Harvey victims while battling cancer.

2 Late Officer Norbert Ramon and other officers helped senior citizens through flooded streets.

3

4

3 Andrea Sutcliffe and Skye assist in the Texas Task Force II's Urban Search and Rescue.

4 Skye rides in the caravan and awaits Andi's orders. (Photos courtesy of Andrea Sutcliffe)

Chapter 5 - Texas Coast Guard to the Rescue

1 Geoff Connor surveys Houston's streets. (Photos courtesy of Geoff Connor)

2 Family rescued calf. Named it Harveigh. He thinks he's a dog.

3 Texas family had 14 rescue dogs - They had to stay when the Hurricane hit. (Photo credit thedodo.com)

Chapter 6 - Holy Responder

1 Father David Bergeron kayaks to those stranded on roads and in houses. (Photos courtesy of Father David Bergeron)

Chapter 7 - Water Reserves Cajun Navy

1 The Cajun Navy drove to Texas' aid.

2 Louisiana volunteers rescue Houstonians.

Chapter 8 - Going Above and Beyond

1. Lt. Bill Fly in his service days.

2. Lt. Fly's house was destroyed during Harvey.

3. Lt. Bill Fly gets help on the rebuilding.

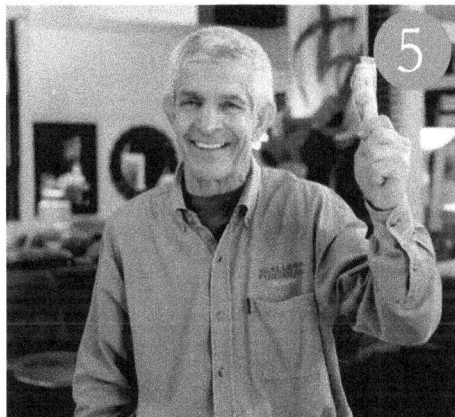

4   Lt. Fly's new kitchen.

5   "Mattress Mack" Jim McIngvale opened two of his Gallery Furniture stores to shelter Hurricane Harvey survivors.

6   Lt. Fly's 100th birthday party.

7   Melanie and Marcus Luttrell with Lt. Fly. (Photos courtesy of Melanie Luttrell)

Chapter 9 - Operation Barbecue Relief

1 Restaurant owner Alex Martin Brennan served over 15,000 meals to victims of the hurricanes. (Photo Courtesy of Brennan's of Houston)

2 Brennan's serves the Houston area. (Photo Courtesy of Brennan's of Houston)

3 Chefs serve at Operation Barbecue.

4 8th Wonder Beer truck rescues people.

5 Ryan Soroko at work.

Chapter 10 - Firefighter Puts Others First

1 Kyle Parry and his fiance, Stephanie Hoekstra.

2 Kyle Parry with puppies.

3 Kyle Parry rescuing people from a bus.

Chapter 11 - God In The Midst of the Storms

1. Rev. Russell Levenson with President George H.W. Bush and the late Barbara Bush.

2. Yehuda Kaploun President of Watergen USA - Creating Water out of air.

3. Rev Russell Levenson with Gary Sinise.

4 K.C. Fox and the Lady General Foundation delivering aid to victims of the hurricane. (Photos courtesy of K.C. Fox)

5 K.C. Fox, Iraq Veteran, Founder Lady General Foundation.

6 Pastor Rudy Rasmus. (Photo courtesy of Pastor Rudy Rasmus)

7 Watergen worked with the American Red Cross and FEMA in the United States to assist people in Texas and Florida by providing clean and safe drinking water in the aftermath of Hurricanes Harvey and Irma.

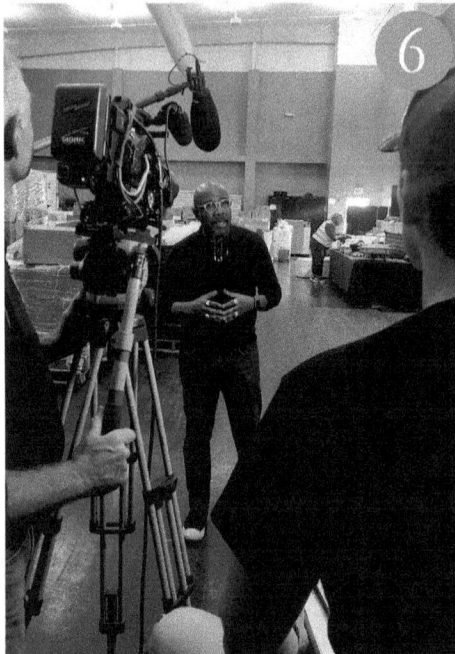

Chapter 12 - Mucking After the Hurricane

1 Donations of art supplies, toys, and games for Bo Duncan's fundraiser. (Photos courtesy of Bo Duncan.)

2 Colin Hoster skateboarding down I-10.

Chapter 13 - Creative Giving

1 Enterprising 4-yr old Caragh raised money by creating artwork and selling it online. (Photos courtesy of Michael Magnus)

Chapter 14 - Texas Strong Tattoos

1 Yahweh approved tattoo parlor. 2 Texas Strong tattoo.

Chapter 15 - Keller Williams Cares

1 KW Cares transports supplies for Harvey.

Chapter 16 - Along Comes Irma

1 Irma hits Florida with massive winds. 2 Rep Ron DeSantis preparing to tangle with Irma.

Chapter 17 - Marc Bell Opens His Heart

Marc Bell opens his heart and home to SOS Children's Village displaced kids. (Photos courtesy of Marc Bell)

Chapter 18 - Operation Linemen Laundry Ladies

Ladies organize laundry services for Florida Linemen.

Chapter 19 - Caring for Island Dolphins

Dolphins were saved during Irma at the Dolphin Care Center.

Chapter 20 - Mercy Chefs

1. The Mercy Chef team.

2. Mercy Chef Ryan & Amber.

3. Chefs Ryan, Bobbie, and Derek serving Irma victims.

4. The Mercy Chefs travel to Santa Rosa after the California wildfires. (Photos courtesy of MercyChefs)

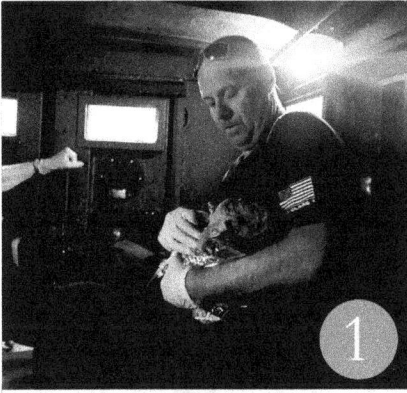

Chapter 21 - Clearwater Police

1. Sgt Scott Myers cradles newborn baby, April, in the back of their bearcat.
(Photo courtesy of Coral Springs Police Dept.)

2. Betty Helmuth and Officer James Fredericks.
(Photos courtesy of Clearwater Police Dept.)

Chapter 22 - Mediterranean Grill Shelters Others

1. Ergin Tek prepares to serve Hurricane Irma victims.
(Photos courtesy of Ergin Tek)

2. Victims of Irma get some tasty cuisine.

Chapter 23 - And Then There Was Maria

1. A Puerto Rican street after Hurricane Maria.

2. Department of Energy Secretary Rick Perry, FEMA Administrator Brock Long, and other senior officials update the media on federal response efforts following Hurricane Irma.
(Photo courtesy of FEMA.gov)

Chapter 24 - Daddy Yankee

1. Singer Daddy Yankee helped raise money at concerts to help fellow Puerto Ricans
(Photo courtesy of Cartel Records)

Chapter 25 - Pastor Bert

1. Pastor Bert Pizarro (center) prays with Maria victims and volunteers.

Chapter 26 - American Radio Relay League

1. Helicopter airlifts victims out for help.

2. Hubert Andy Anderson paints landing strip for airlifts.

3. Hubert Andy Anderson and Carmen Centeno, his interpreter and engineer at the Puerto Rican Dam. They fell in love are now married! (Photos courtesy of Hubert Andy Anderson)

4. Hubert Andy Anderson helping in Puerto Rico.

Chapter 27 - Sixto Mercardios

1 Sixto Mercardios and son Sixto Jr.

Chapter 28 - And Then There Was Ophelia

1 Thomas and Amber Hamilton on the coast of Ireland during Ophelia (Photo Courtesy of Ali and Laura Photography)

Chapter 29 - Prevailing Winds

1. Houston's Mayor Turner answers questions about Hurricane Harvey. (Photo Credit HTV YouTube)

2. Decontamination team members meet with Congressman Michael T. McCaul, 10th District of Texas (far right), and Chuck Brawner, Mayor of Katy (second from right), at the Decon pool and showers at the Base of Operations in Katy, Texas. (Photo Courtesy of FEMA.gov)

3 Texas Rep Gene Green at the Hurricane Harvey flood relief & recovery meeting.

4 Rep Gene Green helping with donations for Harvey victims. (Photos Courtesy of Rep Gene Green)

Chapter 30 - Texas Hospital Association

Ted Shaw CEO of the Texas Hospital Association. (Photo provided by Texas Hospital Association)

PART THREE

HURRICANE MARIA TIMELINE

Saturday, September 16, 2017
The National Hurricane Center predicted that the storm forming hundreds of miles east of Puerto Rico had become Tropical Storm Maria. A Hurricane warning was predicted in the Caribbean by the NHC.

Sunday, September 17, 2017
An Air Force hurricane hunter recorded 75-mph wind speeds and the storm is designated Hurricane Maria. Landfall in Puerto Rico was predicted for Wednesday.

Monday, September 18, 2017
Hurricane Maria experienced the quickest intensifications ever recorded. The NHS warned that the storm developed a pinhole eye that suggested rapid strengthening. By 8 p.m., the storm reached Category 5 status with wind speeds of 150 mph.

Tuesday, September 19, 2017
Landfall was predicted for the following day and Puerto Rico converts 500 schools and other buildings into shelters. 500 U.S. National Guard members were stationed in Puerto Rico along with helicopters.

Wednesday, September 20, 1017

Hurricane Maria made landfall at 6:15 a.m. Sustained winds were recorded at 155 mph. It was predicted that Puerto Rico would receive 30 inches of rain in one day - equal to the amount Houston received during Harvey in three days.

The entire Island lost power and the electrical infrastructure was destroyed.

PUERTO RICO STRONG

"We were prepared for Irma not Maria."
- Governor Ricardo Rosello

23 AND THEN THERE WAS MARIA

"HAIL MARY, FULL OF GRACE, THE LORD IS WITH YE"

After Maria made landfall first on the Island of Dominica and then in Puerto Rico on September 20th, 2017, it wreaked widespread destruction on the Island and its approximately 3.4 million inhabitants. One day before landfall, President Trump said in a tweet, "Puerto Rico being hit hard by new monster Hurricane. Be careful, our hearts are with you-will be there to help!"

The islands in St. Croix in the U.S. Virgin Islands did not get the full fury of the powerful storm. Many had been told by public officials to evacuate or "you will die." Tweets were blasted out. Not since Hurricane Hugo in 1989, had the Virgin Islands taken such a ferocious hit. However, electrical power outages such as during Hugo were not as critical. Windows blew out and there was widespread property damage.

Puerto Rico took a more direct hit. The monster storm was a Category 5 that pounded that Island with nearly 30 hours of unrelenting wind and rain. It was the strongest storm to hit the Island in 90 years. Maria crippled communication networks and destroyed the electrical already weak infrastructure.

Puerto Rico, Spanish for Rich Port, is an unincorporated territory of the United States and a popular tourist destination. As it is not a state, Puerto Rico has a representative but no vote in Congress and does not elect the President or Vice President.

The Island has been suffering from a crumbling infrastructure and financial mismanagement for years. In August 2014, Reuters reported that the Puerto Rico Electric Power Authority was teetering on insolvency. People had been moving away from the Island as a result of rolling blackouts, failing infrastructure and high unemployment. Roads, bridges, dams, ports, hospitals and water treatment plants had been decaying for years.

Puerto Rico was headed for a crisis on any given cloudless sunny day and Maria crippled a beleaguered Island that was already limping along. Following the Hurricane's relentless strike, many of its citizens were without electricity and safe drinking water. The remediation was projected to take months -even years.

In its immediate aftermath, the U.S. Department of Homeland Security's Federal Emergency Management Agency (FEMA) top priority was to provide life-saving resources to Puerto Rico and the U.S. Virgin Islands. It was faced with the ultimate challenge to gain access to the affected areas. FEMA personnel were on the ground on September 21st, 2017 and coordinated with the governors and other counterparts.

The U.S. Coast Guard, who was praised for their efforts by President Trump, were stationed in the Caribbean where they conducted search and rescue operations. The Federal Aviation Administration maintained air traffic control services in San Juan throughout Hurricane Maria's landfall. The FAA was credited with averting potential air traffic disaster for aircraft flying over the Island.

The U.S. Army Corps of Engineers, already stretched thin due to response efforts for Harvey and Irma, had more than 120 responders in the islands during the storms passage. The U.S. Northern Command (NORTHCOM) conducted incident awareness missions with six U.S. helicopters and three U.S. Marine Corps V-22 Osprey aircraft that were launched from the USS Kearsarge Amphibious Readiness group.

Under the leadership of Secretary Rick Perry, the U.S. Department of Energy worked with its partners in response to power restoration efforts. DOE emergency responders were deployed to St. Croix in support of FEMA Incident Management teams. DOE also worked with the Western Area Power Association, the Department of Defense and

FEMA to facilitate mutual aid for the U.S. Virgin Islands and Puerto Rico.

The U.S. Army Corps of Engineers performed power grid restoration and exceeded its goal for generator installation. The Corps previously responded to Texas and Florida as well as California during the wildfires and deserved credit for responding to three major disasters.

There were logistical nightmares that differed from the situation on the mainland United States as there was limited access to Puerto Rico and the U.S. Virgin Islands. "You couldn't drive the trucks to Puerto Rico," said Lt. General Todd Semonite, Chief of Engineers and Commanding General for the U.S. Army Corps, explained at a Pentagon briefing. According to him, the Army Corps had exceeded its goals to restore 30 percent of the Island's power grid by October 31st, 2017.

The U.S. Army Corps had restored 75% by January 2018. Semantic said, "I had guys in Puerto Rico for 157 days." The Corps continued to work months afterwards.

On October 3rd, 2017, President Trump and First Lady Melania visited the ravaged Island and complemented officials. "I hate to tell you but you've thrown our budget a little out of whack," Trump said "And that's fine." President Trump and the First Lady handed out essential supplies and necessities like food and paper towels. Senator Marco Rubio and other lawmakers also visited Puerto Rico.

There were areas outside the city of San Juan that had desperate needs but the roads were impassable in some areas. Both Speaker Paul Ryan and Senate Majority Leader Mitch McConnell committed that Congress would act on a robust disaster funding package.

The American Red Cross deployed its volunteers to the area and volunteers worked around the clock to provide 12.8 million meals and snacks, 40,800 health contacts, 5.2 million relief items and 77.000 water purification filters. More than 2,670 generators were distributed to people with medical needs.

Other not-for-profits swung into action too. The Royal Caribbean sent a cruise ship to evacuate people from the island and to deliver supplies to those affected in the area including St. Croix and St. Thomas.

The death toll has been disputed. Puerto Rico officials originally set the death toll at 64, but a recent Harvard Study based on a survey of household estimated that number at closer to 5000. A judge ordered a release of all death certificates during the Maria time frame.

Businesses and not-for-profits from all over the United States sent aid to the Caribbean. During the One Voice: Somos Live Disaster Relief concert with Alex Rodriguez and Jennifer Lopez, other celebrities like Kim Kardashian West answered calls from viewers who were encouraged to pledge money toward the American Red Cross, Reach Out Worldwide, United Way and other aid groups during the October 2017 telethon.

British billionaire Richard Branson set up a fund to help the Caribbean nations by setting up a green energy fund. He felt that solar energy and other green energy sources could rebuild a stronger more resilient community.

The American Red Cross App features an "I'm Safe" button that allowed users to post a message to their social media accounts to let friends and family know they were out of harm's way. Social media, a curse at times, was a blessing in this situation. Many marked themselves safe on Facebook and posted notices asking for help or volunteers.

24 DADDY YANKEE

"WHAT MATTERS MOST IS HELPING MY COUNTRY"

Ramon Luis Ayala Rodriguez, whose stage name is Daddy Yankee," is a Puerto Rican singer and songwriter. According to the New York Times, he is known as the King of Reggaeton. His album Barrio Fino made history when it became the top-selling Latin music album of the decade between 200-2009. In 2017, he released, in collaboration with the Latin pop singer Luis Fonsi, the hit single Despacito and it became the first Spanish language song to hit number 1 on the Billboard Hot 100 since Macarena in 1996.

As of 2017, Daddy Yankee had won 82 awards and 270 nominations since his rise to fame. He has won 5 Latin Grammy awards, 2 billboard music awards and an MTV Music Video award. He was named by CNN as "The Most influential Hispanic artist of 2009.

He aspired to be a professional baseball player and tried out for the Seattle Mariners of Major League Baseball. No stranger to adversity, he suffered an accident that would prove to be a game changer. Before he could sign, he was hit by a stray round from an AK-47 rifle while taking a break from a recording session. He spent about two years recovering from the wound in his hip and credits the incident with allowing him to focus full time on his career.

He lives in Puerto Rico most of the time, when not touring, and raised over $1 million that he donated to Hurricane Maria and will be divided among Feeding America, The American Red Cross, Habitat for Humanity and local organizations.

Here is Rodriguez's story:

***

"I woke up early in the day on September- I was with my publicist Mayna Nevarez in New York," he recalled. "Hurricane Maria had struck at 5 a.m., and we were desperate to reach our families."

He could not reach anyone. He was being shortly awarded the most demanded artist on the Music Choice TV Channel so he pre-taped his segment for the show. His priority was helping his friends and family in Puerto Rico.

"I was desperate to do something and we tried to reach any organization in Puerto Rico that we could," he recalled. "I knew that people in Puerto Rico were not prepared for the hurricane and so I decided to continue my concert schedule and ask fans to bring water and non perishable goods."

He also performed and produced a video that asked people to bring supplies to his concerts.

"The phones rang non-stop and at a concert in the Coney Island Amphitheater, it was jammed with people shouting VAMOS PARA ARRIBA - which means 'Puerto Rico will rise again."

He added, "We got 4 trucks of goods that one night and I was crying."

He remembered a young Turkish girl who was living in Turkey during the earthquake, brought sanitary towels to his team as she remembered how much it meant to her during her hour of need.

They partnered with Feeding America and helped coordinate trucking food from Chicago, Connecticut and other areas to disburse goods to Puerto Rico.

On September 28th, he returned to his home Island by private jet. "On that day, I arrived to Carolyna, where my family live and I brought with me food, generators, satellite phones, cash and water," he said.

"My house was flooded but it was nothing compared to the massive destruction I saw every where," he recalled. "It's much worse that what we see on tv - the images are horrifying and its getting worse."

He observed that so many bridges were broken and helicopters were needed to deliver food. There was no communication between towns, and a there were no cell phone towers or working bridges to go town to town. Rodriguez helped deliver food, gave ice to the elderly to keep their insulin and other supplies cold, and did all he could. He also wanted to make sure that in the initial phase, that everyone had something to eat and a safe roof over their heads.

He explained that the shelters did not have the same conditions as the United States.

"Not even close," he said.

He observed FEMA and the U.S. Military helping to clear roads and debris but supply distribution was tough. Through church contacts in the U.S., Rodriguez raised money and brought in $200,000 worth of groceries from wholesalers. He oversaw the trucking of bags of rice, beans, oil, salt, water and other supplies to the hardest hit areas.

"I called all the pastors I knew and said, 'I'm sending you trucks with 200 plus bags full of goods and water for your people."

He also bussed in medical supplies for the main hospital in Bayamon. "I tapped every source I could think of and brought in duffle bags full of surgical gauze, bandages, antibiotics and other medical supplies that they were running low on."

In mid October, Rodriguez received a call from the Syrian American Medical Society who wanted to volunteer their services. The group was set up in a 250 bed clinic in Ponce.

As Mayne Nevarez, his publicist said, "You cannot imagine how worried I was about my mom and the other people in Puerto Rico."

She posted on Facebook that she was worried about her grandmother and her family and people she had not spoken to in 20 years contacted her.

"It was for me so emotional to see people who I don't know helping me and one another."

Nevarez said that 44% of the population in Puerto Rico was under poverty before the storm and that now it will be much higher.

"Children cannot get to school and I am worried about the old people including those who have lost everything."

Rodriguez chimed in. The Hurricane brought out the best in Puerto Ricans and help is on the way."

25 PASTOR BERT PIZARRO
"DO NOT BE AFRAID OR DISMAYED"

Bert Pizarro, known as "Pastor Bert," to his friends and congregation, grew up in Brooklyn and Queens, New York but came to Puerto Rico 12 years ago with is wife Zoharis. They were Assemblies of God missionaries. He later started his own church in San Juan where they live with their children.

His Church, Connected Life, cares for the community, helps feed the poor and helps with medical clinics and feeding the homeless. They also host a HopeFest that is a back to school event for kids and provides free haircuts, books and school supplies.

His Church congregation provided essential aid to his fellow Puerto Ricans.

Here is Bert's story in his words.

***

"On Sunday, Sept 17th, the Sunday before Hurricane Maria, I spoke to my congregations: Isaiah 41-10, *"Do not be afraid or dismayed, for I am the Lord your God and your helper,"* he said.

"I spoke that message, got my house ready and told my congregants to get ready as Hurricane Maria is coming," he added.

On Tuesday night, the hurricane began. "Thankfully my kids slept through it. They saw the brunt of it in the morning. I remember telling my wife 'Babe, as soon as we clean up, we will help our neighbors and then we will hit the streets.' "

They began to help their neighbors on the 21st and the 22nd by cleaning up and cutting down trees. By Friday, they packed up the food pantry in the church, made an inventory and made grocery bags, and began to distribute to all the community in San Juan especially in La Plata.

"I went to help elderly people that I knew. I took them to Rio Grande. A pastor friend of mine asked me to check up on his mom and dad in their 80's I took them to my house and they spent the night."

Pastor Bert posted a Facebook video asking for more help, and volunteer teams reached out all from Chicago, New York, Texas. He housed the incoming teams at the district headquarters of the Assemblies of God or at the San Juan YMCA.

He picked up a group of volunteer doctors and nurses and shuttled them to clinics in San Juan, Toa Baja and Utuado. In four days, the team worked with nearly 200 patients.

"When they came to me, it was a leap of faith. But I told them, 'You get here and I'll put you to work.' "

"We started helping one another, neighbors helping one another. We need each other during these time."

22 teams came in, ranging in age from youth to mid 50's, to help from the U.S. - "good people who want to help the people of PUERTO RICO"

'Jesus said love the Lord your God with all your heart, all your soul and all your mine, and love your neighbor like yourself."

"The greatest commandment is to love your neighbor and love God."

He got his electricity back on Nov 22nd but was without power for nearly 2 months.

Bert was driven by the love of God and the love of people. "The stress is overwhelming and sometimes people expect too much, and every morning there is new strength," he said.

He brought people in to do construction. "It's so rewarding to know that God uses me."

"At the end of the day, what matters is people. You can have whatever you want. When you see someone else suffering, you what to help out."

"The most rewarding thing people have said is God has sent you to help us."

26 AMERICAN RADIO RELAY LEAGUE

"I DO NOT CONSIDER MYSELF A HERO. I WAS IN THE RIGHT PLACE AT THE RIGHT TIME" - HUBERT ANDY ANDERSON

The American Red Cross Headquarters suffered the loss of its emergency generator due to flooding. A temporary ARC headquarters was set up with Internet and cell service.

Over the weekend, the American Red Cross (ARC) asked the ARRL for assistance in recruiting 50 radio amateurs who can help record, enter and submit disaster-survivor information into the ARC Safe and Well system. That request was fulfilled. In the nearly 75-year relationship between ARRL and ARC, this was the first time such a request for assistance on this scale had been made.

Resto said radio amateurs also assisted Puerto Rico's Electric Power Authority (Autoridad de Energia Electrica) using 146.52 MHz to dispatch line crews and coordinated fuel deliveries for the authority's offices at the Monacillo Control Center and at several power plants. "The power system is fully shut down for all the island," he said. Drinking water and proper sanitation facilities were in very short supply too. Rest said Puerto Rico needed "everything...solar panels, repeaters, and most important, transmission lines and antennas, some base or mobile VHF/UHF radios, a 1 to 2 kW power generator." Fuel for generators, as well as for vehicles, was running low on Puerto Rico, however.

Radio amateurs in Puerto Rico operated a brisk and busy ad hoc health-and-welfare traffic nets on 7.175 and 14.270 MHz, as did the Salvation Army Team Emergency Network (SATERN) on 14.265 MHz. Nets handled only outgoing traffic. Resto said checking on individuals' welfare typically required attempting to visit them in person, since telecommunications were down nearly everywhere.

Gerry Hull, W1VE, reported that Herb Perez, KK4DCX, in San German, had been operating 6 to 8 hours a day, working dozens of operators, taking numbers and calling families. "I've done at least 200 messages with him," said Hull, who was also active on the SATERN net. Another station in Puerto Rico was operating from solar power.

"Calls to family are very emotional," he told ARRL. "I am getting all kinds of calls day and night for people desperate to hear about family in Puerto Rico, but hams cannot provide inbound traffic." He directed them to the Red Cross website to submit inquiries. "Lots of contesters were helping with their big stations," he said.

U.S. Virgin Islands Section Manager Fred Kleber, K9VV, said the USVI are in much better shape than Puerto Rico. "They really got slammed hard," he said. Kleber said he still had antennas that were not destroyed by the storm and that he can hit Puerto Rico on 2 meters from his location. He also announced plans to deploy some 20 mesh wireless network nodes in the U.S. Virgin Islands.

"We have used every trick in our comms bag of tricks to make stuff work," Kleber said.

Kleber said pictures in the news and social media don't do justice to wholesale devastation, which Caribbean radio amateurs dealt with at their homes and in their communities. He told ARRL late last week that trees, power poles, transformers, and telephone lines were down all over, debris was blocking roadways, and it was taking a long time to get anywhere. He and others had been staffing the emergency communications center 24/7.

Hubert Andy Anderson served in the First battalion 5th Special Forces in Vietnam and was in the military for 22 years. He was a communications specialist throughout his career in the military doing everything from cryptography to radio. His hobby began as a child when he tried to refurbish radios to earn pocket money. His parents were worried that he might get electrocuted.

During Hurricane Harvey, he set up outside Livingston, Texas in his camper. Using his radio for emergency communications, he worked with the Humane Society and rescued about 109 dogs. He also helped in Florida during Irma to communicate with Rescue Operations. There were areas in Florida where there was no cell phone coverage. He helped Irma Search and Rescue with coordination and to distribute emergency and animal supplies.

Anderson later went to Puerto Rico.

These are his words.

***

A friend sent me a text on September 25th, asking me if I wanted to help in Puerto Rico," he recalled. "My biggest concern was finding someone to watch my dogs but I did and we put our paperwork in with the American Radio Relay League and the American Red Cross."

"When the first call went out for radio operators, there were over 400 operators who responded in the first 24 hours," stated Anderson.

He then flew from Indianapolis to Atlanta, Georgia and then he and other ham radio operators loaded all their equipment and flew to San Juan.

"We got off the plane wearing American Red Cross vests and hats signifying we were radio operators," he said. "It was tropical and miserably hot at 90 degrees."

There were more than 24 ham operators from all over the country and they gathered at the Red Cross headquarters and divided into teams. His expertise was antennas.

"Once there, the emergency coordinator for the American Radio Relay League came to me and said there was a problem near a dam that was in danger of breaching," he said. "I went to the Emergency Operations Center where Governor Ricardo Rossello was, along with about 1,700 people including FEMA representatives etc."

He met with the head of the Puerto Rico Fire Department and was told they feared the dam at Guajataca was breeching.

"I volunteered and met engineers there. The Corps of Engineers ensured the next day that the dam was safe. I had sent them coordinates to get there - this was on the 28th and 29th of September."

Anderson added, "Since all the stage pipes had broken, families had dysentery and E Coli in the area I was in. I went into town, bought a bunch of medical supplies, ammonium, etc. with the $1,500 in my pocket- money from the Red Cross. I spent 80% of that on medicine."

"I found out that it was a contaminated water truck that was causing the illness," he recalled.

He went back to San Juan on October 16th. Anderson said, "The Red Cross brought in a psychologist to check us out as it was a very emotional experience for all of us. The worst part of it was seeing the people suffering, trying to do more than they were capable of."

He was cleared by psychologist and came back to Indiana on October 20th.

"I am going to Puerto Rico to help again, but I am going alone," he said. "I will meet other people there. People need our help there."

He said there is extensive ecological damage. "All the flowers that bees need to survive are not there, and there is nothing that will pollinate the population. They are going to have to import millions of bees."

Anderson feels sad for the ongoing road to recovery is slow. "Puerto Ricans are my countrymen and women. There is only one race on this planet: the human race. If we don't help one another, we are doomed."

Many think he is a hero. "I am not a hero. I was in the right place at the right time," he said.

Puerto Rico and the US Virgin Islands both suffered substantial damage from Hurricane Maria, although Puerto Rico took the bigger hit, and it is there that Amateur Radio has begun to fill a huge telecommunications gap.

According to the FCC, service was out for 96% of the cellular telephone sites in Puerto Rico — and was out completely for sites in 78 Puerto Rico counties. In the US Virgin Islands, the overall percentage is 66%.

"The situation in Puerto Rico is very devastating across all the island," Puerto Rico SM Oscar Resto, KP4RF," said Anderson. "Communications via land phone or mobiles are almost null."

"Repeaters are down," he said, "and hams have been using the 2-meter simplex frequency of 146.52 MHz," although he hoped to have a few local ham radio repeaters "working partially with damaged antennas." With police repeaters also down, law enforcement used 2 meters as well.

However, Puerto Rico is strong and the love is there. "We know it's a steep path to recovery," but all things are possible with faith.

27 SIXTO MERCARDIOS
"PUERTO RICO IS STILL IN CRISIS"

Sixto Mercardios left Puerto Rico in 1999 and joined the U.S. Marine Corps. He later worked for Marine Security Forces at the White House from 2000 and traveled with President Bush and President Clinton. He now works at the State Department of Protocol.

In his words, he tells of the lasting effects of Maria in Puerto Rico.

***

"When Hurricane Maria happened I was in my house in DC, but I made sure my parents had every supply they needed - water, food, ice. The neighbors who had refrigeration who were good friends of mine made sure my friends were ok. My mom is a diabetic and her insulin has to be kept in the fridge," he recalled.

"My friends had a working phone in Puerto Rico, and I was able to call them and ask about my parent's house and the community. My friend Edward went to my parents' house and put them on the cell phone to talk to me."

He followed the news 24/7 and at least 7 people died in Toa Baja his home town, northwest of San Juan. "This town is a coastal town. It has a lot of restaurants and schools. There used to be a naval base there that shut down, so it was a pretty basic, empty town before the hurricane," he said.

His aunt Milagros lost everything she owned on the first floor of her house including her car.

"She actually described to me how rats were floating looking for dry land, were climbing all over the soggy furniture in her house... The rats are dangerous," he recalled.

"Many people died in Puerto Rico from Leptospirosis - that is a disease caused by rats urine if it gets in your water, food... very serious disease. There is treatment for it - sometimes doctors fail to recognize the symptoms. If you don't get the right treatment, you die," he added.

(Weil's disease is a form of a bacterial infection also known as Leptospirosis that is carried by animals, most commonly in rats and cattle. It can be caught by humans through contact with rat or cattle urine, most commonly occurring through contaminated fresh water.)

"Once the power went out, all refrigerated foods went bad like meat and fish that needs to be refrigerated. The food ends up in a dumpster, which becomes a haven for rats'"

He has an understanding that if it gets too uncomfortable, his parents will come to the U.S. "My father is a tough guy- keeps my mom safe - but there is no running water in many houses and even the traffic lights are not working in Puerto Rico so there are lots of accidents. It's very dangerous."

"Thousands of police have not shown up at work as they have not been paid. They are calling in sick. It's a major crisis."

"During the hurricane, when they are running the hospital Vieques off a generator, people were stealing the fuel from the generators," he said.

Still today there are homes with no roofs.

In the San Juan area, the houses are concrete. In the ghettos and in the mountains where people live, the houses are made of wood. People in the mountains are waiting on FEMA to write checks for their losses," he added.

In old San Juan he estimated 10,000 employees are trying to get back to work but with no electricity or water. There are no jobs.

"It was difficult for the government to control the relief effort initially as the roads were closed with debris, electrical wiring, plus no diesel fuel," he added.

While he feels things are improving, recovery is a long way off. "In the mountains, the situation is still dire. People in the mountains didn't get help until U.S. military went there a month later," he said.

He said it will be decades to get people on the Island back on their feet. "Our hearts are totally broken."

PART FOUR

HURRICANE OPHELIA TIMELINE

The tenth and final consecutive hurricane and the sixth major hurricane of the 2017 Atlantic Hurricane season, Ophelia was regarded as the worst storm to affect Ireland in 50 years.

It first formed on October 6th, 2017 and gained strength in two days as it drifted North and southwards.

Saturday, October 11, 2017
Ophelia became a major hurricane. It was designated at a Category 2.

Tuesday, October 14, 2017
It intensified and progressed toward Ireland and Great Britain where it battered the coast of Ireland.

Friday, October 17, 2017
Ophelia struck western Norway with wind gusts up to 70 mph.

28 FINALLY OPHELIA

Ophelia was first reported to be barreling toward the United Kingdom with winds of 140 mph. It's landfall was predicted to coincide with the 30th anniversary of the Great Storm of 1987 which occurred on October 15th. It was powerful, and it intensified as a cyclone. The anniversary coincidence seemed liked an ominous warning.

After it made landfall around the Southeast coastal area, several hundred thousand people were without power which was not fully restored until two weeks later. The estimated cost to the insurance industry was $2 billion.

By the time it hit Ireland, it had the distinction of being the first ever severe weather alert for the entire country. The Irish National Meteorological Service, Met Eireann, warned that the storm would be a danger to life and property and that most of the damage would come from flooding.

National Hurricane Scientist Eric Blake tweeted "Ophelia is breaking new ground for a major hurricane as typically these waters are too cool for anything this strong."

Ophelia was in many ways a typical tropical cyclone with a tight spiral of cloud, powerfully strong winds and a cloud-free eye.

But what set it apart from other Atlantic hurricanes was its direct route to Europe. While hurricanes do sometimes take a circuitous route westward across the ocean and loop back again towards Europe, this one took a shortcut.

Ophelia began as a rather innocuous looking group of clouds in the Atlantic Ocean, several hundred miles southwest of the Azores and roughly on the same latitude as Morocco or northern Florida - yet even at this stage it was unusual.

Most named storms in the Atlantic are generated in warmer waters much further south and, as such, they are generally driven across the ocean by the easterly (blowing westwards) trade winds. They eventually dissipate as they curve north into the Atlantic or make landfall in the Caribbean, Mexico or the US.

In Ophelia's case, moderate atmospheric shear (changes in direction and strength of wind with height) and relatively cool sea surface temperatures meant it took several days to develop the well-defined low pressure centre, strong winds and spiral clouds of a hurricane. Then, instead of traveling west, like most Atlantic hurricanes, Ophelia began to head northeast.

This can be explained by the position and strength of the mid-latitude jet stream, an atmospheric feature that plays a major role in determining the weather over Western Europe.

When its path loops north over the UK it can produce stable warm conditions in the summer (as in the record-breaking heatwave of July 2015), and bright cold days in the winter.

When its path west to east is more direct, it guides low pressure storm systems across the UK and Ireland and can be responsible for the rapid strengthening of storms in a short period of time (described colloquially by forecasters as a "weather bomb"). It is this that produced such a rapid change in direction for Ophelia.

Such waves on the mid-latitude jet stream are not unusual, however, the combination of both the jet's and Ophelia's position produced the conditions to guide the ex-hurricane toward the British Isles.

Ahead of Ophelia's arrival, the UK had a weekend of unseasonably balmy temperatures thanks to warm tropical air driven northwards. This is partly due to the winds circulating around the Ophelia low pressure centre, but also the positioning of the jet stream helping to draw air up from the tropics.

On Monday, Oct 16th, much of the UK looked far less like a hurricane had arrived, and much more like the whole country had been put through a rosy Instagram filter. The sun was particularly red at dawn and throughout much of the day the whole sky glowed a yellowy-orange.

An increased number of particles in the atmosphere scattered light preferentially from the blue end of the spectrum, leaving the more orange and red colors to reach our eyes.

This effect was partly thanks to the southerly winds on Ophelia's eastern side, which transported Saharan dust and smoke from Iberian forest fires. In fact, several flights over the UK were forced to make emergency landings when smoke could be smelt in the cabin.

OPHELIA DIDN'T STOP THE LOVE

THOMAS AND AMBER HAMILTON
TIE THE KNOT
"JESUS IS OUR FOCUS"

So what happens when your happy day coincides with the arrival of a hurricane and its aftermath? Despite winds of up to 80 mph battering Northern Ireland and towns closing shops and transportation services, Thomas and Amber Hamilton's wedding went on with the show.

Amber is from Wisconsin, and her husband Thomas is from Coleraine in Londonderry, Northern Ireland.

An American with a can do spirit, Amber was not going to postpone her wedding. The couple is adventurous, and so were their wedding photographers, Laura and Ali Moore.

Laura Moore is in partnership with her husband, Alastair "Ali" as photographers from the northwest of Ireland. They love to photograph couples in love in natural settings. A family of three, they live with their son, Freddie, who is two.

This is their story in Laura's words.

***

"Jesus is our focus, and we are total apple geeks," she said.

She explained that Amber and Thomas had seen their website and contacted them to do their photos. "They liked our style," Laura said. "We like to capture the mood using natural elements."

Little did they expect natural elements to include the remnants of a major storm.

The Hamilton wedding ceremony was held on October 16th in the City Hall in Portrush, County Antrim, Northern Ireland. They braved the weather at Ramore Head, a rocky headland that is at the tip of the Peninsula. According to Laura, there are fabulous cliff walks at the top with 360 degree views, but the limestone cliffs posed a challenge in the high winds. Despite the rocky terrain, they headed up the cliff walk.

"It was refreshing to take the photos, and the Hamiltons really didn't care how they looked," she recalled. "They wanted to capture the magnificent outside and he beauty of Moorehead, Cliff."

She said that they were safety cautious and did not get close to the cliff's edge. As the weather deteriorated, the bride had been concerned about the climb and how the photo shoot would turn out .

"Amber was a bit worried in the days leading up to the wedding, but there was no way they were going to change the date," she said. "They had too many guests coming from States and others traveling to attend as well."

The shoot went really well and the photos were great. She added, "Obviously it was not ideal weather but there was something really romantic about the shoot." The lighting was raw and lovely.

"When they got back to the reception and told their friends and family we were climbing the rocks at Ramore Head, they probably thought they were crazy."

Undaunted, the happy couple even danced to Ophelia by the Lumineers.

THE POLITICAL FACTOR

29 PREVAILING WINDS
BIPARTISAN COOPERATION

The prevailing political winds pre-hurricane were brisk. Congress faced headwinds in session. Bickering, obstructionist behavior and division was rampant. Yet for a brief but memorable period of time, politicians reached across the aisle and worked together to address the trio of national emergencies. For one shining moment the **H Factor** was apparent.

Senator Ted Cruz said on CNBC News, that the focus is search and rescue - not political sniping. "I'm not going to worry about political sniping. My focus here is on the tragedy that is unfolding, on the people whose lives are in jeopardy and the people who need help," Cruz said in an interview on Fast Money Halftime Report.

Cruz also emphasized that hurricane funding is an important federal responsibility. "The damage is going to be very extensive," he said. "The combined cost of destruction of property in Hurricanes Irma and Harvey could range from $200 billion to $250 billion. These are stunning price tags - sticker shock for the Federal Government."

Under President Trump's leadership, Congress passed a $90 billion disaster aid package in February 2018. The bill provided help for citrus farmers in Florida who sustained more than $760 million in losses. It also provides $2.7 billion for schools impacted by the storm. $10.4 billion was allocated for the U.S. Army Corps of Engineers to use for construction projects. Some of the funding was earmarked for Puerto Rico to rebuild its power grid.

The Texas and Florida delegation pulled together. Both Governors Abbott and Scott received high praise for their leadership efforts. Senator Marco Rubio's staff hosted Irma Recovery Assistance Centers. They were available to help residents sign up for assistance by FEMA.

"The people of Florida are resilient, and I know together we will get through these tough times. My office and I are here to help you," he said in a press release.

In Houston, Mayor Turner and the Houston Police Department received kudos for his strong leadership. Rep. Sheila Jackson Lee called for $150 billion in aid to help the Houston area. Lee has represented the downtown Houston area for decades. She was often at the George R. Brown Convention Center, turned shelter, and she gave a report on what she was seeing at the time among her constituents.

"I just came back from the northeast part of the district, where they were rescuing about 50 people, including elderly that were frail, babies, moms and others that were disabled, but these were resilient people who are waiting and really said 'we will wait it out.' "

"And we're trying to restore people's lives. But we need to do it with federal resources."

Congressman Michael McCaul's response to the disaster was successful as there was strong coordination between all levels of government. He credited the seamless response as saving thousands of lives.

He said that when waters are rising, there is national focus but that they must work hard not to forget others after the waters have receded. As Chairman of the House Committee on Homeland Security, he is in a unique position to oversee the recovery and mitigation efforts in his home state.

He planned to focus on the Addicks and Barker reservoirs that quickly filled with water up to capacity and forced the release by the Army Corps of Engineers to release waters from the structures to preserve their sold integrity. The subsequent water released flooded thousands of homes. The subsequent flooding has been the subject of numerous lawsuits and controversy.

McCaul is taking the lead on a solution. "A breach of the Barker or Addicks Reservoirs would have sent a tsunami of water through Buffalo Bayou and into downtown Houston." He later explained. The solution according to McCaul will not be easy or cheap.

"This is probably the highest priority in the state in terms of flood control for the number of people who would be affected and the number of people whose lives and whose homes we can save if we do simply what the government intended to do 70 years ago."

He feels the money is there, and that the question is how quickly can it be done. McCaul, whose grandfather survived the Great Storm of 1900 in Galveston, takes this responsibility to spotlight Texas and those in need personally. "My grandfather was a young child, and he managed to ride out the storm on a rooftop." The hurricane left between 6,000 to 12,000 fatalities as the storm surge inundated the entire island. His family story left a lasting impact on his can-do spirit.

He continues to hold hearings on the ongoing recovery and rebuilding effort.

McCaul later advocated for the cutting of red tape to speed up recovery efforts. "One of the lessons we learned and discussed during a post-hurricane hearing was the necessity to streamline federal funding directly to the local level so those most in need receive help as soon as possible. Instead of the additional layers of approval, we should be able to provide Community Development Block Grants directly to the City of Houston and Harris County so our local governments can use funds without delay."

In September 2017, Lt. Gov. Dan Patrick - Texas - asked Senators to study a series of interim legislative charges directly related to Harvey issues. It said in the Katy News, "Since Harvey made landfall, I have said this Texas-sized storm will require a Texas-sized response. My goal is for our state to become national model in handling every aspect of disaster, and the interim changes I'm releasing today are the next step in achieving that goal."

The Texas-sized generosity was again on display when Texans for Dan Patrick announced it was donating $200,000 to the Rebuild Texas Fund, which was established in August 2017 by Governor Greg Abbott in collaboration with the Michael and Susan Dell Foundation and the

OneStar Foundation to help with recovery and response. The Dell Foundation contributed $36 million to the fund with the long-term vision for the recovery of affected areas.

It's worth noting that there were many first responders and efforts from non-affected states. Nashville, Tennessee firefighters deployed to help with Harvey and Irma. Others came from across the U.S.

Recovery continues to be an ongoing, slow and arduous process in Florida and especially Puerto Rico. There is Federal monies available and politicians, for the most part, seem to be putting a priority on those suffering in the aftermath. Indeed, the **H Factor** appeared to be working when the Historic Tax Reform - Tax Cuts and Jobs Acts - was passed on December 22nd, 2017. It passed the Senate 51-48. A miracle.

The H Factor at work.

AN INTERVIEW WITH MAYOR SYLVESTER TURNER OF HOUSTON

Were you surprised by the massive public response you got from people all over the country offering help?

"I would not say I was surprised. Houston has always been a city centered on neighbors helping neighbors. It's a city where people are more than willing to help each other. We saw that with their response to Harvey, the generosity of the people who responded quickly and supportively was truly amazing. I am certainly glad that people all over the country were persuaded to follow suit.

Was there a particular story/person that really struck a chord with you?

Some striking photojournalism was produced from the news coverage of Harvey, and the ones that stick in our memories most are the photos of first responders and volunteers using their arms or private boats to carry people to safety. The beauty of those selfless acts endures.

How did FEMA help the people in Houston? Are there still people trying to get back in their homes?

One of the ways FEMA provided necessary support was with immediate funds. Hundreds of thousands of people received SNAP cards for sustenance, even those who would not regularly qualify for the program. There are still many people out of their homes, and a lot of damage that must be addressed. As of February 20th, we still had about 3,433 households living in hotels. So despite what has been accomplished, there is truly a lot of work that needs to be done. Thankfully, we have some exceptional people in the city working together to continue rebuilding and taking care of all Houstonians.

What makes the Houston spirit special?

I am always proud to say that one in four Houstonians was born outside of our country, and it's this diversity that has made ours a very welcoming community. Our people are focused on building relationships, not walls. These connections point to a strength that is unmatched anywhere else, and that certainly came out in the face of this disaster. No other city could have done what we did as quickly, together, and I believe that we have faced with this storm has made us an even stronger, more resilient Houston.

Does it make you proud to be Mayor Houston and watch what a great job the first responders did?

I am very proud of the first responders and how the people of the city reacted. I will never forget the brave actions of the first responders from Houston as well as the many volunteers that were of service to their neighbors during the storm. There were many people who risked their lives and gave their time and resources to come to the aid of others. We know here that neighbors helping neighbors is what Houston is all about, and I can't thank them enough.

As a Democrat, you worked with both Democrats and Republicans during this crisis response. Including Ed Emmett. Are there other leaders you worked with as well and what stood out in this bipartisan effort as important?

A natural disaster of the size of Harvey, which brought more rain than any American city in modern record has withstood, does not discriminate. This was made very clear to us, it was a storm that had no dividing lines. The Mayor is not elected on a partisan ticket, but beyond that, a natural disaster of that magnitude did not give any concern to the party of the people it affected, and therefore neither did the leaders who responded to it.

Who or what motivates you in times of crisis?

The number one job of the Mayor is to guarantee the safety of the people. The second is to protect their property. Actually, 77% of the budget is set aside for police and fire. So when we are having to make decisions quickly, that number one duty was the first concern behind each one. What is most important now is to continue looking out for our most vulnerable neighbors to create an even more resilient city that is ready to face the next storms that are sure to come.

How did your family survive the hurricane?

My family was thankfully just fine during the hurricane. We are very grateful, and much more fortunate than many. Now, we are working on making sure that the people who need help receive it, focusing especially on the elderly, people with special needs, that are still recovering and whose homes continue to need urgent repairs.

What life lessons have you learned from handling this storm to prepare you for the next one?

As we move forward, it's important to continue having faith in each other to create a stronger Houston and keep an eye out for a brighter future. We are still working hard for Houstonians, and it's important to maintain the relationships with the people around s that will help us keep working towards a city of opportunities that is stronger, more powerful, and more ready. We have been put on notice with this storm and previous storms, and it is our utmost priority to take steps to mitigate future challenges and costs.

Why did you decide not to evacuate Houston for Hurricane Harvey, and what was the decision making process to reach this conclusion?

After realizing that the problem was going to be heavy rain, not a storm surge or extremely high winds, it was clear that to keep Houstonians safe and to minimize the danger they would face, the best decision was not to evacuate. We truly had no way of knowing where the rain would be strongest, where we could tell people to go, and how to help them if they were not at home. Considering the magnitude of this storm, and the flawed evacuation attempt for Hurricane Rita in 2005, it would not have been reasonable to ask 6.5 million people to get on the roads. We had a very devastating situation with Harvey, but if an order to evacuate had been given it is very probable that a lot more lives would have been lost. This hurricane was a historic event for Houston, and one that I am confident we can continue to rise

AN INTERVIEW
WITH REP. MULLIN

A terrific example of bipartisan politics in action, or the so-called **H Factor**, was when Democratic Representative Gene Green, 29th Congressional District of Texas and Republican representative Markwayne Mullin, 2nd Congressional District, Oklahoma came together to assist after Hurricane Harvey.

Green said, "The Houston spirit is the Texas spirit and I worked with my Republican colleagues to come together in times of disaster."

"At short notice, we all worked together as a bipartisan delegation for the good of the District and the good of the state."

In Representative Mullin's words, this is their story.

***

Gene Green told us you were helpful. The friendship is bipartisan and illustrates that politics goes out the window in times of crisis, can you elaborate on the joint response effort with Gene?

Gene and I have developed at friendship and have worked together multiple times on several pieces of legislation and we sit on the same committee. But we have a thing in Oklahoma called Oklahoma Standard and every time we have had a disaster, our friends from the south, they always seem to just flood up here. From the bombing to the tornadoes that have hit, and it was really simple when I saw that area was hit for me to reach out to Gene and say how can we help you. What's great is, I'm Cherokee and I contacted Cherokee Nation and my friends over there jumped all over board. They went down there for a week and ended up staying several weeks. It was a great partnership. You know when your neighbor is in trouble you don't ask them if it's a Republican or Democrat, you just help them.

Were you surprised by the massive public response you got from all over Oklahoma offering to help you and your neighboring state of Texas?

No, not at all. As I said it's the Oklahoma Standard. I would expect no different.

What is your reaction to the mobilization of emergency personal and FEMA it appears to be well orchestrated?

Well, you know, fortunately and unfortunately, unfortunately we have had a lot of practice at it. Fortunately, every time we do we get better at it. And so, from the response from the White House, to the response of an agency, to the response from the local authorities. Having the ability to coordinate and coordinate fast that's not by accident, that's by design and even if it happens, which is probably not if, it's when something like this happens again, you are going to be able to see us respond better.

Was there a particular story or person that really struck a chord with you that wanted to help?

We have 19 tribes within our district, 19 separate in a sense, 19 separate government. That's because each tribe is considered its own government and out of 19, I can't think of one that wasn't reaching out to me personally asking how they can help. I was just recently with a fire and rescue team down in Southeast Oklahoma and they were talking about, they had a team of people from Oklahoma that was in a number of 230 plus people. They were naming organization after organization after organization that were coming straight from our Oklahoma. So, I don't have one, I have as our state as a whole. Even Love's Truck Stops sent down sent down trailers full of water to different colleagues of mine, not just Gene Green, but other colleagues of mine that needed water in their district. You had Love's Bottling Company that was doing the same thing and I didn't have to contact any of them. They were contacting me saying if you know of anyone that needs help, let us know.

What is it about Oklahoma that sets the Oklahoma Standard?

It's because we went through it so many times, its neighbor happy to help neighbor. We aren't at the practice of just waiting for someone to come to our aid when we are able to help ourselves. It's just like my dad instilled in me when I was younger, you never walk by a problem and leave it for another man when you are able to do it yourself. My dad is not the only one who instilled that in me, obviously we can see that's been passed down by generation to generation within the families.

Does is make you proud to watch what a great job the first responders did, and ordinary people did, neighbor helping neighbor in trouble times?

It makes you proud to be an Oklahoman, it makes you proud to be from the United States. Absolutely.

As a Republican, you worked with Democrats and Republicans during this crisis response, are there other leaders you worked with as well and what stood out in this by part effort that is important?

Cooperation. No one was asking the question "how can we get paid" from the Tribes, to corporation, to individuals, to the state. No one cared about that, it was just get the job done. And I don't hear about how much it cost me or how much it cost us even to this day. What I hear about are the stories of how people from Houston were so thankful we were there. One story I heard was the group o the 230 plus individuals from Oklahoma that all went down there they got a 15 miles section of people they were supposed to evacuate, they said they were stationed in a parking lot in a mall and they were sleeping in their trucks. And a church found out about it and the whole time they were there, came up there every single day, picked up all of their dirty laundry and would stuff notes and there was a fire chief that was in the group and he showed me the notes that were given to them from the people of Houston. Those are stories that stick out to me, it was the response that this person could be my mother, could be my father, or brother, or sister and you would expect someone to do the same if they needed your help.

Does politics go out the window in times of crisis?

Yes, definitely. Who cares if you are Republican or Democrat or Independent. Who cares if you socially agree with me or don't socially agree with me. The fact is, is that you are in need of help and there is still enough decency in our country to say we are going to help you.

Who or what motivated you in times of a crisis?

I don't know, I think it was just the way I was raised. We make decision based on two things, life experiences and the way we were raised. Ive needed help before in my life and there has always been someone there willing to help. And I was raised that you are always supposed to help someone in time of need and I think that is pretty standard.

Do you look to faith for guidance?

Always, I got saved when I was 20 years old. I was raised in the church, but I dedicated my life to the Lord when I was 20 and seems like a habit to always go to the Lord in the time of need. But the relationship that I have, I'm thankful for the good times and I'm thankful for the bad times and I pray for endurance when I need it the most.

How was your family owned business, Mullin Plumbing involved in the relief efforts of Hurricane Harvey?

We did everything we could to provide supplies and needs and we also had guys that responded. But even the guys that responded were volunteers. We didn't assign anybody to go. In fact, I think all of our employees would have gone down there, but we had things we had to do up here too. But I've seen my employees inside our company do this over and over again and none of them asked for a write up, to get over time, none of them asked to even get paid. They actually say we will take off on our own course, we don't expect to do that. Our office has been through several of these. From tornadoes up in Oklahoma City to loading here back home and every time our office is doing things before I even have to ask them to do things.

THE FLORIDA RESPONSE ALSO WAS BIPARTISAN

Ambassador Francis Rooney represents Florida's 19th Congressional District and is a successful businessman who brings decades of private sector experience to Washington.

He and his family started Rooney Holdings, Inc. (RHI), a diversified, international group of companies based in Naples, Florida. Since 1984, RHI has created jobs and economic opportunities in Southwest Florida and throughout the United States.

One of the company's subsidiaries is Manhattan Construction Company, a diversified construction group founded in 1896.

Significant projects around the United States include the Presidential Libraries for both George H.W. Bush in College Station, Texas, and George W. Bush in Dallas, Texas; the Dallas Cowboys stadium; the U.S. Capitol Visitors' Center; the Walter Reed Army Institute for Research; and the International Terminal at Hartsfield-Jackson Airport in Atlanta, Georgia.

In addition to his business career, Rooney and his family have a longstanding tradition of public and community service. He was appointed by President George W. Bush to serve as U.S. Ambassador to the Holy See from 2005 to 2008, and has also served on numerous public and private boards, including Naples Community Hospital, the Florida Gulf Coast University Foundation, the Center for the Study of the Presidency and Congress, and the Advisory Commission of the Panama Canal.

A graduate of Georgetown University (A.B. 1975) and Georgetown University Law Center (J.D. 1978), Rooney has honorary degrees from the University of Notre Dame (2006) and the University of Dallas (2010). he is a former member of the District of Columbia and Texas Bars, holds a U.S. Coast Guard 100 Ton Masters License (sailing endorsement), and is a lifetime member of the National Rifle Association.

He and his wife, Kathleen, live in Southwest Florida and have three children: Larry, married to Porscha; Michael, married to Frances; and Kathleen; one grandson, Beckett, and one granddaughter, Bergen.

Rep. Francis Rooney in his words.

***

Where you surprised by the massive public response you got from people all over the country offering help?
"A lot of people came to volunteer even from as far away as Alaska, Nevada and the MidWest. It was heartwarming to see -the great human spirit, People stayed for several weeks. It was organized by the local Red cross Makes me feel good, a local distribution facility Clive Daniel opened its Ft. Myers warehouse doors to the Red Cross as a place to store relief supplies. Soon, Red Cross emergency response vehicles from around the nation poured into the warehouse to help distribute clean-up kits, mops, rakes, tarps, bleach and more into the communities hit hardest by Irma. Not only did they donate the warehouse space, but Clive Daniel drivers and trucks jumped in to support the Red Cross relief operation, helping to deliver these supplies."

Was there a particular story/ person that really struck a chord with you?
"I was truly inspired by the volunteers who organized St Matthews House. Donations from Southwest Florida and several states were distributed by St. Matthew's House to hundreds of people in need of direct assistance after Hurricane Irma. I even went there to distribute aid and to thank the workers for all the work they do"
For thirty years St. Matthew's House has provided innovative solutions to fight homelessness, hunger, substance abuse, and poverty in Southwest Florida. St. Matthew's House is a 501(c) (3) which does not depend upon government funding, and its

100% donation model allow all operating expenses to be covered by unique social enterprises. Find out more online at www. stmatthewshouse.org.

How did FEMA help the people in FLORIDA.. Are there still people trying to get back in their homes?

"Everyone is now back in their homes , there are some roofs still damaged. FEMA did amazing job we organized in my district special FEMA fairs, with the Small Business Administration and Government Housing Agency, everyone in one room a one stop shop to help people in need. There were even translators for people who did not speak English to help them fill out forms so they could get their lives back on track

Did you go out and help on rescue missions in Florida what was that moment like?

"I and Vice President Mike Pence and U.S. Sen. Marco Rubio joined a largely Hispanic crowd at a church, Ministerio Internacional El Rey Jesus Naples.

People came from all over the country. My job with with VP was to load supplies that had been donated onto trucks to get to outlying areas. We worked flat out for 5 hours There were 500 people there to see the VP.

VP Pence is a decent human being a moral leader, we are fortunate to have a man like this as a VP.

One of great thing about storm the way it brought people together people whose homes partially damaged helping people who had lost everything heartwarming to see people power.

On Sept 14th, 2017 President Trump, came to Naples to survey the extent of Hurricane Irma's destruction, and to thank public safety services and meet first-hand with victims of the most powerful hurricane to hit the United States sine Katrina in 2005."

When he flew over Bonita Springs on Marine One, the president's helicopter cruised low enough for him to see screen doors, siding and other debris strewn across carefully laid out subdivisions.

"I was part of the delegation, with Senator Marco Rubio, Governor Scott and Vice President Pence and First Lady Melania Trump. We drove into the Naples Estates neighborhood, witnessed downed trees, ripped out street signs, tarp-covered roofs and totaled mobile homes. Empty gas stations advertised they had no fuel.

President Trump did a walking tour of Naples Estates, a retirement community made up of manufactured homes nestled among the region's many golf courses. He even distributed sandwiches on the estate.

President Trump stayed 4 hours, walked around different neighborhoods. The people were so thankful he was there- his visit was so successful and confidence boosting to people who had lost a lot during the storm. He truly cares"

Does it make you proud to to watch what a great job the first responders did, and ordinary folks did neighbor helping neighbor in troubled times?

"I could not be more proud, watching people from all across the country, neighbor helping neighbor, rich and poor pitching in to help"

As a Republican you worked with both Democrats and Republicans during this crisis response. Are there other leaders you worked with as well and what stood out in this bipartisan effort as important?

"On Dec 21st, 2017, The House of Representatives passed $81 billion in new disaster recovery funds to provide for relief for Hurricane Harvey and other natural disasters, including crucial flood mitigation projects. Texas and Florida congressional delegations joined forces to significantly increase the original $44 billion funding request from the Office of Management and Budget. In addition to more FEMA, housing, business, agriculture, infrastructure and economic development funding, the measure includes $12.5 billion to help communities protect against future natural disaster and prevent repetitive costs. We were united on saying what we needed to have to protect our areas. It was a united front. We got all the money we need. We were happy"

Does politics go out the window in times of crisis?

"By and large everyone chips in it was not a partisan issue "

Who or what motivates you in times of crisis?

"Crises bring people together in a unique way for better or worse."

Do you look to faith for guidance?

"Of course, I was Ambassador to the Holy See. We all have to look to God for moral values.

30 TEXAS HOSPITAL ASSOCIATION

"GOD HAS TAKEN CARE OF ME"

During the storms, hospitals faced unique challenges. The Texas Hospital Association was equal to the task, and many lives were saved.

Ted Shaw is the CEO, who leads the 450 member association in advocacy and member services for the THA family of companies.

The Texas Hospital Association:

- Develops and maintains a sound organizational structure by monitoring and evaluating the continued strategic and financial success of the family of companies.

- Provides leadership and strategic counsel to the board of trustees, membership and staff. Represents THA membership to regulators, state and national lawmakers and the public.

- Maintains relationships and communications with external entities that affect hospitals and health systems in the state.

- Translates the board's policy decisions into actionable strategies and tactics, ensuring the association exceeds the expectations of the membership.

- The Texas Hospital Association this week estimated that as many as 75,000 hospital employees experienced losses and damage from Hurricane Harvey, both the storm and subsequent flooding.

- The association, which is based in Austin and represents more than 85 percent of the state's acute-care hospitals and health care systems that combined employ some 365,000 health care professionals, announced Sept. 5 that it is contributing $1 million to a special assistance fund for the affected employees.

- THA, along with other state hospital associations and health care organizations across the country, established the hospital employee assistance fund and reported that it has drawn donations from hospitals, corporations, an independent supporters across the country, including a $50,000 contribution from the American Hospital Association.

"Throughout the storm the days following, we witnessed firsthand the dedication of our health care workforce," said Ted Shaw, THA's president and CEO.

"Many of these individuals stayed committed to their work, knowing their families and property were at risk. While hospital administrative personnel, nurses, and other staff train for unspeakable disasters like Hurricane Harvey, their preparation and focus ensured the safety and continued operation of facilities even as the waters rose and the lights went out. Now, it's time for us to take care of the caregivers."

Hospital employees who work inside the disaster areas designated by FEMA are eligible for assistance.

Meanwhile, THA is asking the Texas hospital community for help to raise more donations. "The effects from the devastation wrought by Hurricane Harvey will be with us long after the water recedes and the media spotlight fades away," Shaw said, "but our support for the thousands of dedicated Texas hospital employees who selflessly cared for the sick, elderly, and vulnerable under truly challenging conditions will remain steadfast."

In his words:

***

What were the challenges and successes that Harvey affected hospitals and governmental partners experienced in responding to the storm?

"In any crisis like this the challenges are unexpected Epic storm (Harvey) 5 days long - 64 inches of rain largest rain event in history in the United States. Bigger than Katrina, I lived through Katrina too. Katrina was much more focused. Dynamics different New Orleans at sub sea level, it surrounded by dykes the levees broke different kind of storm.

The problems in Texas massive size of storm and rain spread across a much wider area.

Hurricane Harvey Impacted 180 hospitals miracle of all of this only 10 closed and they only closed for a week.

The way we responded to Hurricane Harvey, our people had to be there 24/7 for a week. The employees and patients stay in the hospital, people with nowhere to go have to be sheltered too - we make room for people in cafeterias and physicians offices.

There is not distinction between between rich and poor when your living home is flooded."

How often do staff from THA have major training sessions to prepare for hurricanes?

"We prepare annually all type for all types of crisis, mass casualties, Ebola, hurricanes. We have conferences, update our annual plans, share them on an annual basis.

One lucky things for us this time - we were able to build on what happened in Louisiana, and in NY Hurricane Sandy, those who shared with us there plans made it that such are streamlined for us."

What life lessons can be learned from the training?

"Be prepared. Be prepared for what you don't expect. Don't panic. Help each other.

The life lesson is bad things are going to happen, work together to solve it."

There were many dramatic stories of people arriving in dump trucks in groups of 30 or more or being dropped off by Blackhawk helicopters at hospitals, is there a particular story that resonated with you?

"You have to be proud of people/our staff were incredible, good things happened - people found ways to get people in trouble to the hospital. People left their families, staff not knowing the status of their own homes.

It was extraordinary how all 50 states contributed to a fund set up by the TEXAS HOSPITAL ASSOCIATION - We took care of 5400 hospital employees, raising 2.4 million dollars to help them rebuild their damaged homes."

Does it make you proud to to watch what a great job the first responders did, and ordinary Texans did neighbor helping neighbor in troubled times?

"I could not not be more proud. People came in alligator boats and fishing trucks, going through neighborhoods to rescue sick people. Sometimes they left people in places they should not have been. A number of people were dropped off in Park East Texas at a hospital that was closed- they broke in and stayed for a week. We called the governor who sent the national guard there to make sure everyone was safe."

What challenges do hospitals face during the storm?

"One of the challenges during the storm: people on dialysis could not get in to have dialysis. Centers were closed and they got dumped in hospitals. They were much sicker because they didn't get dialysis and ended up in ICU or surgery.

This was exasperated by the storm, particularly when you don't think a storm is going to last 5 days.

The doctors, nurses and housekeepers stayed in hospitals, 24/7 - whether they had to sleep in patient rooms or cots - they were there to take care of patients.

We get to be able to touch people lives in a positive fashion.

You hear about a storm approaching, you bulk up supplies like food and water. Generally, you have enough for 3 days.

When we began to run short of supplies, we were blessed by the

The Hospital Corporation of America, who had logistics - planes, helicopters, trucks - to bring in supplies and restock the hospitals with what they needed. They would stage supplies out of storm area.

In the midst of this, water is very important for cleanliness in hospitals. We had 2 or 3 situations where city water was fouled. So we had to have water trucked in. Christies Hospital had a way of purifying water on site.

You need tap water for dining, cooking, cleaning, washing. You need water for the air conditioning too. Hospitals can never use rain water. It's just not pure.

Normally in hospitals, we have supplies inventory, which lasts a day and a half. We bulk that up in times of hurricanes. We have to have back up have plans in place for how we restock. When water is too high you have to get in to restock by helicopter or boats. When the water recedes, you can bring in trucks.

If you lost power, that's a crisis - every hospital has backup power generators. During Katrina, I was in a hospital as an administrator in East Jefferson. The US Navy flew it in the power.

We all work together in these times. Prejudices and competition goes out the window. All except taking care of your follow man."

What is special about TEXAS spirit?

"Texas spirit we don't ever quit. Whether or not it comes from any religious position, if we don't have faith, we lose our hope. If we lose our hope, we quit.

In Texas, we don't quit. We keep pushing forward. I am very proud of the fact, we had huge damage but everyone was helping their neighbor.

Our hospitals were back in full scope 10 days later. It's good people on the ground that make plans. The dedication of your caregivers was extraordinary.

Even if you, like me, don't put hands on patients - as an administrator, we all dive in to help.

One of my employees, Carrie Kroll, among her many other responsibilities, got in a position to answer all the calls during the storm for the hospital and staff. For 10 days she took calls nonstop. When we tried to get her to hand off, she said she could not as she is so dedicated and committed."

Are you prepared for the next big one?

"We are going to be better prepared. We did debriefs with Homeland Security and other hospitals. We published a paper on it. Communication is something we need to be better at."

Tell us about the special Houston Medical Center.

"The Houston Medical Center is connected underground to other hospitals in the area. They transport patents, supplies, etc. underground.

This time round, they had submarine doors in the tunnels so water did not get in. They had moat-like walls around the hospital. (There are other hospitals in Texas that have underground tunnels)."

How important was faith to all of you on the front lines of the Hurricane?

Do you have a favorite passage of scripture that resonated with you all during Hurricane Harvey?

LUKE CHAPTER 10:25-3

The Parable of the Good Samaritan
Have Mercy and Help your fellow man

25 On one occasion an expert in the law stood up to test Jesus. "Teacher," he asked," what must I do to inherit eternal life?"

26 "What is written in the Law?" he replied. "How do you read it?"

27 He answered, "'Love the Lord your God with all your heart and with all your soul and with all your strength and with all your mind'[a]; and, 'Love your neighbor as yourself.'[b]"

28 "You have answered correctly," Jesus replied. "Do this and you will live."

29 But he wanted to justify himself, so he asked Jesus, "And who is my neighbor?"

30 In reply Jesus said: "A man was going down from Jerusalem to Jericho, when he was attacked by robbers. They stripped him of his clothes, beat him and went away, leaving him half dead. 31 A priest happened to be going dow the same road, and when he saw the man, he passed by on the other side. 32 So too, a Levite, when he came to the place and saw him, passed by on the other side. 33 But a Samaritan, as he traveled, come where the man was; and when he saw him, he took pity on him. 34 He went to him and bandaged his wounds, pouring on oil and wine. Then he put the man on his own donkey, brought him to an inn and took care of him. 35 The next day he took out two denarii[c] and gave them to the innkeeper. 'Look after him,' he said, 'and when I return, I will reimburse you for any extra expense you may have.'

36 "Which of these three do you think was a neighbor to the man who fell into the hands of robbers?"

37 The expert in the law replied, "The one who had mercy on him."

Jesus told him, "Go and do likewise."

POSTSCRIPT

On July 18th, 2018, Texas Gov. Greg Abbott honored dozens of first responders and community leaders who were designated as "Harvey Heroes." At the crowded event held at the Lone Star Flight Museum, Abbott said, "When we come together as one, there is no challenge we cannot overcome."

He added, "More money has been received faster than any other catastrophe in state history - more than $30 Billion so far.

Abbott paid tribute as well to the thousands of people who put their lives on the line to make a difference.

Many organizations are involved with the rebuilding process including Team Rubicon. Founded in 2010, Team Rubicon relies on the skills of military veterans and first responders to deploy response teams to emergencies.

With 75,000 volunteers, Team Rubicon has responded to 259 disasters in the U.S. and around the world. A portion of the generous donation by President Trump has been earmarked for Team Rubicon.

The Caribbean islands of St. Maarten and St. Martin, post Irma, are well on their way to recovery. Almost one-third of the islands buildings were battered by winds of up to 182 mph. The high winds also blew off portions of the roof at the new Princess Juliana International Airport.

Irma's price tag, in all, was estimated at $3 Billion in that area. The tourism industry is slowing recovering although some mega destination resorts remain closed.

In the Florida Keys, rebuilding operations are in full force. Recovery operations in this battle tested zone began almost immediately. Cruise shifts have returned to the port of Key West and the undersea Park, Key Largo, has resumed glass bottom boats and snorkel tours. Other Keys attractions like the Florida Keys Aquarium have reopened.

Florida's strength and resilience is on full display during the 2018 summer vacation season.   Better times with blue skies is definitely on the horizon.

In Puerto Rico, the island is green again and the beaches are open for business. A popular tourist friendly town, Rincon, on the West Coast is visitor ready. Some of the top ten beaches are as glorious as ever.

There are certainly many areas where the recovery/rebuilding process is slow. The roadways in some areas are in bad shape with deep potholes. The electric and cellular services are spotty in poorer neighborhoods. Therefore, the Island desperately needs a revival of tourism as an economic engine.

An October 2017 New York Times Opinion Piece by Juan Giustu-Cordero summer it all up in one sentence: "In Puerto Rico, We Invented Resilience."

Throughout 2017, incredible acts of exemplary courage was on display for the world.   America, the land of the free and the brave, showed its United resolve after horrific natural disasters and tragedies - shootings, wildfires and the like.

People of faith across America exhibited teamwork and unification on a common mission of survival.   Ultimately this lack of division, was the **Hurricane Factor** in practice.

Another question loomed "How Strong is your faith?" Sometimes, it seems, we need reminders that faith is the answer in times of adversity. Faith is necessary in coping with our daily storms as well.

"We cannot choose to avoid adversity, but we can choose how we will respond." And if there is one lesson, it is this: We have more in common than what divides us. People, for the most part, are inherently good. It's fine to agree to disagree, but for several shining moments in 2017, agreement didn't matter. We all were reminded that life is fragile. We need each other. We can work together, and Americans are the beacons of a free world. If only we could remember daily that we need one another - **The Faith Factor.**

ACKNOWLEDGEMENTS

Many friends are blessings in my life, some new, some long term - who make my life richer. I wish to acknowledge those who have had my back during social media attacks, the fire and just in general. In no particular order, Dianne Kube, Keith Schiller, Kristina, Josh Campbell, Steve Smith, John Butler, Kris Perry, Travis and Liz Lucas, Cammy Jones, Anita Perry, Mike McMahon, Mike Campi, Mike Sharkey, Jaime Gonzalez, Chris Farrell, Tom Fitton, Joe and Rachel Dillon, Mark and Stacy Serrano, Tony Shaffer, Tony and Marie Sayegh, Carolyn Poole, Pastor Paul, Lisa Swayze, Eileen Littlefield, Albert de Prisco, Jeff Colyer, the Trump Tower staff, John McCutchen, Carola Myers, Martha Blecher, Mickey Nelson, Frank Torchia, Rob Arlett, Neil Cavuto, and Geir Haarde.

Thank you to Jono Anzalone of the American Red Cross for shepherding me around at the George R. Brown Convention Center during Harvey. He introduced me to his amazing team of volunteers and made my experience especially meaningful.

A big shout out to Kathryn Milofsky who tirelessly researched stories and facilitated the interview process. A talented television producer, and a fiery Irish lass!!!

Also a thank you to Mickael Damelincourt and the DC Trump Hotel staff and USSS George Georges and the staff at Four Seasons Austin. Julien Farel Salon, and Andre Chreky Salon, Brad, Hope, Kamal, and Pepe.

But most importantly and above all, thanks be to the Lord Almighty, who got so many through troubled times and got this book through production.

ABOUT THE AUTHOR

Mica Mosbacher, widow of the 28th U.S. Secretary of Commerce, Robert Mosbacher, is a political strategist and author of *Racing Forward: Faith, Love and Triumph Over Loss;* and *The Hurricane Factor: Storm Side Patriots, One Voice, One Nation, One God.* She has held national roles in five presidential campaigns and is presently an Advisor of the 2020 Trump Campaign, and an advisory Board of the Women For Trump Coalition. She is a frequent guest on Fox News, Fox Business, BBC World News, BBC Radio, LBC and CBC Radio, APR Radio and other international news channels.

Active for two decades in political fundraising, she has hosted or co-hosted numerous fundraisers for GOP candidates. She was an RNC National Finance Co-chair in 2012. In 2007, she served as Inaugural Chair for Governors Rick Perry and David Dewhurst. She served as 2008 Women For Mcain Co-chair, 2012 National Co-chair for Secretary Perry's presidential election, and as a co chair Women for Cruz.

In addition, Mica has co-chaired numerous charitable events including a record fundraiser for the M.D. Anderson Cancer Center, Houston Ballet, World War II Museum, Archdiocese for the Military and Texas Association Against Sexual Assault, (TAASA).

Active in education, she helped initiate the Best Friends Program founded by Elayne Bennet in Houston area public schools. She was appointed to a six-year term on the University of Houston Board of Regents by Governor Perry and served as Vice Chair.

She has been humbled to receive many awards including induction into the Greater Houston Women's Chamber of Commerce Hall of Fame along with Barbara Bush and multiple excellence in journalism honors by her peers. For her work on advocating for passage of funding for sexual assault prevention programs and other related legislation, she was named Philanthropist of the Year by TAASA. The American Hospital of Paris Foundation honored her with their Public Service Award presented by Ambassador Howard Leach at the Embassy.

In April 2011, Houston Mayor Annise Parker and the Houston City Council designated a "Mica Mosbacher Day" in her honor for her initiation in a prominent public art installation in Houston focused on tolerance with sculptors by world-renowned Jaume Plensa. She was awarded two damehoods including the Royal Order of Francis I.

In 2010, she was commissioned by the Foreign Ministry of Iceland with approval by the State Department as Honorary Consul General of Iceland for Houston and Central Texas. She served in that capacity for eight years. She currently serves on the advisory board of Turning Point USA and the London Center for Policy Research.

Mica resides in Austin, Texas and Washington, D.C. and is active in many conservative and faith-based organizations. Mica has two grandsons and is a member of Holy Trinity Church, in D.C. Mica is a fifth generation Floridian and grew up in Houston, Texas.

Follow Mica

http://micamosbacher.com

Twitter:

https://twitter.com/mosbacher_mica

Facebook:

https://www.facebook.com/MicaMosbacherAuthor